W0016604

From
a Sabine
Jar

Lowell Edmunds

The University of North Carolina Press • Chapel Hill & London

From a Sabine Jar

Reading Horace,

Odes 1.9

The paper in this book meets the guidelines for
permanence and durability of the Committee on
Production Guidelines for Book Longevity of the
Council on Library Resources.

96 95 94 93 92   5 4 3 2 1

Library of Congress Cataloging-in-Publication Data
Edmunds, Lowell.
    From a Sabine jar : reading Horace, Odes 1.9 /
Lowell Edmunds.
        p.   cm.
    Includes bibliographical references and index.
    ISBN 0-8078-2008-3 (cloth : alk. paper)
    1. Horace. Carmina. Liber I, 9. I. Title.
PA6411.E36 1992
874′.01—dc20   91-22215
                                                           CIP

Frontispiece: Monte Soratte (Soracte), without snow,
looking east from Castel S. Elia. The town in the
foreground is Faleria. The mountains visible to the
left of Soratte are the Sabini. (Photograph by Charlotte Sullivan)

Contents

· · · · · · · · · · ·

Preface

. . . .

About seventy articles, notes, or parts of books on Horace, Odes 1.9, called "The Soracte Ode" after the mountain named in its second line, are in print, not to mention dozens of commentaries in several languages. The author of a recent article on this poem, published in a major journal, speaks of the work of his many predecessors in terms of "general and particular misconceptions," "associative fantasy," "curiosities of explication," "more than one level of misunderstanding," and "obtuseness." Let us imagine an intelligent outsider (hereafter "O") who knows nothing about classical scholarship except this article and the fact that seventy-odd bibliographic items already have been published in respectable journals and by esteemed presses. O might at first think that the vituperative author was a genius heaping condign scorn on the pygmies who had foolishly attempted to say something about the poem before him. Having finished the article, however, O will not have found any signs of genius and will seek for some other explanation for the author's pride. Has the author made a theoretical breakthrough? On the contrary, O will find that literary theory is discussed and dismissed in a single footnote. What O may not grasp is that the conventions of publication in classics require the detection of previous error as a starting point. It must be exposed in all its ugliness and then replaced with new truth. Thus, having cudgeled his predecessors, the author of the recent article discovers that the flumina of stanza 1, which were frozen rivers all down the centuries, are really icicles hanging from the trees. What did he leave for the next scholar who wrote on this poem except to change the meaning of the adverbial phrase *nec iam*, traditionally "no longer," to "not yet," so that the previous author's icicles melted and became flowing streams?

The present study of *Odes* 1.9, though it is offered to classicists as well as outsiders, does not enter the discussion in a moment defined by the history of this poem's interpretation within classics. Developments that have taken place outside of classics, culminating in the well-known crisis of the text, require an extraphilological orientation, if not for "the progress of the field" of classics at least for its possible presence in a wider context of literary studies. *Odes* 1.9 is here the occasion for investigating the possibility of reading a Latin poem according to certain principles and methods not widely used in classics. This approach asks, can these "foreign" methods contribute anything to understanding the poem? And also, can this exercise offer anything to the theoretical discussion from which it started?

For some readers, the adjective "theoretical" in the preceding sentence will be cause for alarm. A typical classicist's response to literary theory has already been glimpsed in the survey of a recent article above. The same author insists on a poem so ironclad that it is almost impervious to reading of any sort: Mount Soracte "exists within the domain of the poem; it is part of an ordered sequence of words. As such, it is not accessible for appraisal outside the sequence, nor can anything be predicated of it beyond what is stated or clearly implied by the words in the sequence." In fact, we should leave the ode alone. After twenty-two pages the author closes with a warning: "To supplement the text [that is, the sequence of words] is easy and mistaken; but such additions divert us from the text itself, which, discreet and subtle, must be left in its silences." Other readers will laugh aloud not only at these statements but probably also at the suggestion, at the end of the preceding paragraph, that a classicist could contribute anything to theoretical discussion.

The classicist's qualms about theory are not entirely unjustified, as I have argued in the introduction to *Classics: A Discipline and Profession* in Crisis?[1] Much or most literary theory has emerged from the reading of modern literature, which is often accessible without a large dose of peripheral information. The reader is already at the periphery of a modern text. Ancient texts are not accessible without knowledge of ancient languages, which can never be as perfect as the knowledge of a modern, spoken language. Ancient texts reach us via a long process of copying by hand, during which they were altered by error and emendation. For these reasons the reading of an ancient text must be supported by philology, in the form of an apparatus criticus and a commentary. Other kinds of historical information are often necessary, too. Theory, the classicist feels, will never shorten our distance from ancient texts. Only hard work—and philology seems harder than theory—can bridge the distance.

The classicist is partly right and partly wrong. Certainly the traditional historical route to the text must be traversed. But, once there, at the text or as close as possible, what rules out a theoretically based reading? This further step might be dismissed as irrelevant to the project of classics as currently understood, but that it is irrelevant tout court would require another kind of argument, in fact a theoretical one. As such an argument is not likely to emerge from classics, the present enterprise is free to proceed, at least as far as classics is concerned.

The model for the present reading of Odes 1.9 is an essay by Hans Robert Jauss on a poem in Baudelaire's Les fleurs du mal.[2] This essay was published originally in 1980 and in English translation in 1982 in a collection called Toward an Aesthetic of Reception. Jauss starts with Hans-Georg Gadamer's principle of the historical separation of reader and text as itself productive of the meaning of the text. Gadamer used

1. Edited with Phyllis Culham and Alden Smith (Lanham: University Press of America, 1990).

2. It is the second of four poems in Les fleurs du mal, all entitled "Spleen" (see Baudelaire 1961, 79, no. 76). Thus Jauss sometimes refers to this poem as "Spleen II."

the word "horizon" to describe the hermeneutical situation. The horizon of the interpreter includes his or her prejudices and other limitations. Gadamer described understanding as a fusion of the interpreter's horizon with the historical horizon of the text. Jauss took up the word "horizon" and made it famous in the expression "horizon of expectation," so famous that it was already used by German sportswriters in the mid-1970s. Jauss emphasized the difference between the reader's horizon of expectation and the work itself, between the reader's previous aesthetic experience and the "horizonal change" demanded by the reception of the new work. Neither Gadamer's position nor even Jauss's is here defended at the level of theory, however. Rather, Jauss's method is applied in an experimental spirit to the reading of an ode of Horace.

The Jaussian reading is really a series of three readings, the first perceptual or aesthetic, the second interpretive, and the third historicist, attempting to recover the horizon of expectation of the original audience. The first three chapters of this book perform three such readings. Each chapter begins with a discussion of the kind of reading it performs. Though the philosophic basis of Jauss's method is diametrically opposed to the historical positivism of philology, the sequence of readings allows for and even demands the accommodation of historical information. For this reason the Jaussian method may be more useful and acceptable to classicists than others now in fashion.

What will become apparent, however, even in the first reading of *Odes* 1.9, is that this method reverses the usual procedure of classical scholarship when it is concerned with an aesthetic question like the unity of a poem. The practice of classical philology requires, in the first place, analysis, that is, the separation of the poem into parts, then the focus usually on some subset of these parts, then usually the determination of new facts concerning the subset, which are the evidence for the scholar's argument, and, finally, demonstration of the poem's unity on the basis of this evidence. Philology and history precede aesthetics. In Jaussian hermeneutics the initial aesthetic reading is never replaced by, but in fact determines, the second reading, the interpretive one, in which philological and historical information is likely to come into play. The Jaussian inverts the philological approach. The movement of the first three chapters of this book thus brings into ever sharper focus the confrontation of Jaussian reading and philological analysis, as reading itself, in contradistinction to analysis, becomes a criterion by which the two approaches can be distinguished. In the Jaussian approach the unity of the poem appears in the reading; in philology it appears, as it were, outside the poem, in the analysis. The fourth chapter takes this confrontation as its theme and provides a survey, necessarily partial, of the scholarship on *Odes* 1.9.

And yet philology's claims to its understanding of the poem are never here denied, and, as will be seen, the Jaussian model must in fact be modified for the reading of this and presumably other ancient poems. A certain characteristic movement of philology, the quest for comparanda, leads in the fifth and final chapter to a dimension of the poem that had escaped the Jaussian readings and thus to a deeper questioning of the model.

The inspiration for this monograph came from a course in Horace's odes that I taught at Rutgers in the spring semester of 1989. The first three chapters were written, and the fourth and fifth were prepared, during the same spring and in the summer, partly in Baltimore, Maryland, and partly in Highland Park, New Jersey. In the latter place, I was living in the home of Kenneth Wheeler. His study was a most congenial place for Horatian meditations. His hospitality was both a practical and a scholarly boon. After the fall semester was over, I returned to my project, now in a home of my own and in a study created by Susan Edmunds, and was able to finish the writing during the Christmas vacation. The manuscript was submitted for publication on January 19, 1990, and twice revised on the basis of useful sets of comments from anonymous referees.

I am grateful to John D. Baird, Daniela Battisti, John Davis, Hannah Edmunds, Susan Edmunds, Carolyn G. Koehler, Nita Krevans, David Lachterman, Alessandra Bertini Malgarini, Maria Theresa Moevs, John Pollini, Kathleen Slane, Alden Smith, Carl P. E. Springer,

Charlotte Sullivan, Robert Wallace, E. L. Will, Roger Woodard, and James E. G. Zetzel for various kinds of help, and to the staffs of the Douglass and Alexander libraries at Rutgers for helping me to gather all the writings on Odes 1.9. Parts of my readings of the poem were presented to audiences at Pennsylvania State University and at the University of California at Los Angeles during the fall of 1989, to which I am indebted for challenging responses. I also wish to thank Charlotte Sullivan, who took the photograph that appears as the frontispiece of the book.

The text of Horace from which Odes 1.9 is quoted in the opening pages of this book and from which parts of this and other poems are quoted elsewhere is the Teubner edition of S. Borzsák, *Quinti Horatii opera* (Leipzig, 1984). It is reprinted here by permission of B. G. Teubner Verlagsgesellschaft, KG, Leipzig. The translation by Cedric Whitman has been published in *Fifteen Odes of Horace* (Cambridge, Mass., 1980) and is reproduced by permission of Lee Miriam Whitman-Raymond.

Highland Park, New Jersey
May 1990

Abbreviations

· · · · · · · · · · ·

Abbreviations of ancient and modern titles are generally consistent with those of *L'année philologique* and with the second edition of the *Oxford Classical Dictionary* or the OLD. OLD refers to the *Oxford Latin Dictionary*, ed. P. G. W. Glare (Oxford: Clarendon Press, 1982); "Lewis and Short" to Charlton D. Lewis and Charles Short, *A Latin Dictionary* (Oxford: Clarendon Press, 1879).

Horace,
Odes 1.9

• • • • • • • • • •

Vides ut alta stet nive candidum
Soracte, nec iam sustineant onus
silvae laborantes, geluque
flumina constiterint acuto?

dissolve frigus, ligna super foco
large reponens atque benignius
deprome quadrimum Sabina,
o Thaliarche, merum diota.

permitte divis cetera, qui simul
stravere ventos aequore fervido
deproeliantis, nec cupressi
nec veteres agitantur orni.

quid sit futurum cras, fuge quaerere, et
quem fors dierum cumque dabit, lucro
adpone, nec dulcis amores
sperne puer neque tu choreas,

donec virenti canities abest
morosa. nunc et campus et areae
lenesque sub noctem susurri
conposita repetantur hora,

nunc et latentis proditor intumo
gratus puellae risus ab angulo
pignusque dereptum lacerto
aut digito male pertinaci.

Translation by
Cedric Whitman

. . . .

You see how deep Soracte stands in snow,
A hoary blaze, the laboring forests cringing
 Under the load, the rivers standing
 Pinned in their course by piercing ice.

Heap logs in plenty on the grate, melt off
The cold, and tilt the crock up by both handles,
 Good revel master, pour the four year
 Vintage out with freer hand.

Leave all the rest to the gods; once they have laid
Asleep these winds that now go brawling over
 The boiling sea, no more will cypress
 Shiver and flail, nor aged ash.

Let be what comes tomorrow, reckoning
Pure gain whatever gift of days your fortune
 Yields, and in youth be not disdainful
 Of love in all its sweetness; dance,

While yet no sorry white head nods upon
Your springtime shoulders; look to the piazza,
 The pleasure walks, the hushed whisper
 By nightfall at the trysting hour;

When a girl's laughter happily betrays
Her hiding place, lurked in a secret corner;
 Then plunder a trinket from her finger,
 Or languidly protesting arm.

1

. . . .

The
Jaussian
Readings

1

. . . .

First
Reading

The first reading, limited to the horizon of aesthetic perception, is not literally first but is rather a reconstruction of a first reading. The reader is not naive but has read other lyric poems, in Latin and in other languages, and is, by the standards of his or her own culture, an educated man or woman. Certainly he or she can read Latin well enough to read the poem. In the first reading, however, this reader suspends detailed historical information and refrains from interrupting the reading to do research. Standard grammars, commentaries, and dictionaries will be the only supports, and information from such sources will have been absorbed in the actual readings that go to make up the idealized first reading. Therefore, the references to dictionaries and grammars in what follows have a status different from the one they would have in a philological discussion. These references are not arguments from authority for particular points but indications of the earlier empirical stages of reading that resulted in the final first reading here presented.

In practice, it is most unlikely that anyone would undertake a project like this one without already having read something about Horace and the ode under discussion. No doubt Horatian scholars will be able to detect in this first reading adherence to one or another commentator, to one or another scholarly position on C. 1.9 already in print. (The choice of Borzsák's text, which entails an important decision about the punctuation of the first sentence of the ode, is a patent example.)[1] Again, such inevitable influences are not a covert parti pris that the reader of my first reading should construe as implicit participation in philological controversy. Rather, they are what might be called the unconscious of the first reading, which, in its strict aesthetic focus, forgets them in order to conform with the method. In this chapter, I shall have cited only four articles on C. 1.9, three of which are something like first readings and therefore comparable with my first reading.[2] But in the fifth chapter of this study, the relation of my interpretation of C. 1.9 to nineteenth- and twentieth-century scholarship on this ode will be spelled out.

Vides ut . . . ? "Do you see how . . . ?" An unidentified speaker poses a question to an unidentified addressee. The poem is dramatic in the sense that there are two characters. What is the relationship between them? This question is not answered in the first stanza. The speaker proceeds to describe a cold winter scene. By the end of the first line the reader sees, or hears, that Horace has written an Alcaic hendecasyllabic, and, by the end of the first stanza, that Horace is imitating a certain Alcaic stanza and a particular poem of Alcaeus (338 Lobel-Page). Horace's imitation of Alcaeus is some large part of his means of representing to the reader the relationship between the speaker and the addressee, which will be that of senior and junior symposiast, of older and younger man. This imitation belongs to a code by which Horace communicates with the reader (the code includes versification and poetic diction), unless the reader imagines that the speaker, as distinguished from Horace, is dropping allusions for the addressee, as distinguished from the reader, in what might be called metalyrical

---

1. And also the choice of the reading *lacerto* in line 23. In principle, the Jaussian approach would open the possibility of a return to this textual problem within the aesthetic horizon of the first reading. In practice, I shall not return to this particular question.

2. First readings: Klinz 1967; Esler 1968–69; Moskovit 1977. For the sound patterns of the poem, which might properly have had a larger place in my first reading, see Baneke 1963–64.

fashion (cf. "metafiction"). The reader is thus engaged, by the end of the first stanza, in two relationships, that between speaker and addressee, and that between Horace and himself.

The difference between the first stanzas of Horace's and Alcaeus' poems is thus a clue to the reader. The opening lines of the latter's are:

ὕει μὲν ὁ Ζεῦς, ἐκ δ᾽ ὀράνω
χείμων, πεπάγαισιν δ᾽ ὑδάτων ῥόαι . . .
(1–2)

Zeus rains. From heaven a great
storm, and frozen are the streams of water . . .

Although the comparison of the two stanzas is necessarily incomplete, as the third and fourth lines of Alcaeus' poem are missing, some things are clear. Whereas Alcaeus begins with a verb in the third person singular (ὕει), Horace begins with a verb in the second person singular and thus immediately establishes a relationship between the speaker and an addressee. Alcaeus begins with Zeus raining and with a storm descending from the heavens. In Horace, Zeus has disappeared, and the storm is over. From the first stanza of Alcaeus (as known to us, to repeat, in two of its four lines), Horace has taken only the frozen rivers.

Horace's winter scene is indeed marked by frozenness, by arrest. Ice arrests the rivers, the weight of snow constrains the toiling tree branches, and Mount Soracte is covered with deep snow. A certain monotony pervades the description, as Horace enumerates the items of the landscape, placing a noun, in the nominative each time, at the beginning of each line: Soracte (2), silvae (3), flumina (4). Horace thus seems to have developed a single element of Alcaeus' scene, and here is a clue. But to what is it the clue? The answer will gradually emerge in the first stanza, but this is not the only question the reader faces. The first element of the scene described by Horace, the focus of the scene, is Mount Soracte. It "stands out,"[3] both for the addres-

---

3. Lewis and Short s.v. sto I.B.9.

see, in the description, and for the reader. Does it also stand for something? In the context of imitation of the Greek poet, Alcaeus, is Soracte
presented as specifically Roman? Where are the speaker and the addressee in relation to the scene the speaker describes?

While a first stanza inevitably poses some questions just because it is first, this stanza also has a perceptible design and com-
pleteness that emerge from its versification. Before I proceed with
the reading, however, I can anticipate the distinction between reading and philology that will be developed in the fourth chapter. From
the viewpoint of philology, the versification is a matter of metrics,
and in handbooks and commentaries a scheme like the following is
presented:

$$1 \quad \stackrel{\smile}{-} - \smile\smile - \; \| \; - \smile\smile - \smile -$$
$$2 \quad \stackrel{\smile}{-} - \smile\smile - \; \| \; - \smile\smile - \smile -$$
$$3 \quad - \smile - \smile - \smile - -$$
$$4 \quad - \smile\smile - \smile\smile - \smile - -$$

This scheme then receives commentary: The first and second lines
are the Alcaic hendecasyllabic. It has a caesura, that is, a regular break,
after the fifth syllable. The first syllable can be either long or short but
is usually long.[4] The typical nucleus of Aeolic meter, the choriamb
($- \smile \smile -$), appears after the caesura. The third line is the Alcaic nine-
syllable line. It is without a regular caesura but has a tendency to place
words of a certain kind in the center: a long monosyllable and a spon-
dee ($- -$) or vice versa or a word of the metrical shape: $- \smile\smile -$. The result
is that a word break is common after the sixth syllable and that the
center of the line has the weight of grouped long syllables. The last
line is brighter and lighter with five short syllables as against two in
the preceding line. Further, it has a cascading rhythm, opening with
a dactylic movement—a dactyl ($- \smile \smile$) followed by a choriamb. And
the last three syllables, echoing the last three of the preceding line,
have a clausular effect. Everything that has just been said is true and

---

4. The statistics have long since been gathered (see Bonnvia-Hunt 1954) and
are repeated in metrical handbooks and sometimes in commentaries.

must have been absorbed by the would-be reader, but to conceive of the stanza in this way may be to believe that Horace thought and composed in these same terms, line by line. The commentary of Kenneth Quinn, for example, states that the third line of the stanza is "an abbreviated form" of the first and that the fourth is "made up from the second halves of the previous lines."[5] Can such a description aid a *reader*? Quinn's analysis is based, I believe, on the *visual* marks, the brevia and longa that he provides in a scansional pattern like the one set out above, and is unrelated to anything one experiences when one reads the poem. In the fourth chapter, I shall show the rather large role that visual strategies play not only in metrics but also in other kinds of philological interpretation.

If one reads the poem and listens to it, one finds that the stanza is arranged in four units of sound *and* sense. The first unit runs from the beginning of line 1 to the caesura, the second from after the caesura in line 1 to the caesura in line 2, the third from after the caesura in line 2 to after the weighty center of the third line, and the fourth from there to the end. The fourth of these units is especially perceptible in the first three stanzas of this ode: consider the syntactical linking of the ends of the third and fourth lines in each of these stanzas in such a way as to frame the fourth unit:

geluque
acuto?

Sabina
diota.

cupressi
orni.

The first three units of the first stanza are as follows (the conventional symbol ‖ indicating a caesura, ◊ a sense pause):

1   2
Vides ut alta ‖ stet nive candidum

5. Quinn 1980, 140.

3

Soracte, ◊ nec iam ‖ sustineant onus
silvae laborantes ◊

The position of the monosyllabic *stet*, after the caesura, emphasizes this word and reinforces its semantics—the word itself stands there—and thus reinforces the effect of the visual image of Soracte, the subject of *stet*: the mountain "stands out." Likewise, *sustineant* gains emphasis from its place after the second caesura, and the point of this emphasis is reinforced by *laborantes* at the end of the sense unit: the trees "are toiling." The woods are thus to some degree personified, and their *onus* is not only the physical weight of snow but also a burden, a care.[6] The snow that covers Soracte and its trees and presumably the ice in the rivers, too, are the tokens not only of atmospheric cold but also of cares the speaker sees in them and calls the addressee's attention to.

Because Roman houses did not have the kind of windows from which a landscape could be observed, the addressee is called upon not to behold but to visualize, to picture the aftermath of the storm. The mountain is a mental image for the addressee, as it is for the reader, and the speaker's personification of the trees is thus the particular form in which he wants the addressee to picture them. In this way, the speaker's question ("Do you see. . . ?") is a rhetorical one. It tells the addressee something: "the trees are burdened, like you (or us)," or "the trees are burdened, unlike you (or us)."

To digress again (and for the last time in this chapter), a peculiarity of the second line focuses the methodological issues discussed above. In the second unit, sound and sense do not concur. A sense pause occurs after *Soracte*, momentarily isolating *nec iam* ("no longer") before the caesura. Without some prior knowledge of metrics and of the metrics of this poem in particular, the reader would not have noticed this detail of versification. (As said, this first reading is an ideal one.) And yet the detail, from the metrical or philological

6. See Lewis and Short s.v. *onus* II.B; *OLD* s.v. *onus* 5.

point of view, is not important enough to warrant comment, and, in the dozens of scholarly discussions of this poem, one will not find it mentioned. It is the *reader*, who attempts to hear the speaker of the poem, who notices the curious emphasis on *nec iam* and takes it as a clue, though to what he or she does not yet know. Like the personification of the landscape, it must have something to do with the relationship between the speaker and the addressee. It does not, in any case, communicate anything immediately from Horace to the reader.

In the fourth and concluding sense unit, word order encloses the rivers in the "sharp cold," the ice, that has arrested them:

4
◊ geluque
flumina constiterint acuto?

Constiterint, in the center of the fourth line, is the intensive form of *sto*, the verb already emphasized by its place in the first line. As the rhythm of the fourth line is clausular (with repetition of the pattern of the last three syllables of the preceding line: ˘ ˉ ˉ), so *constiterint* completes the picture of arrested nature. Horace, or the speaker, has thus given a precise focus to Alcaeus' winter landscape, and he has done so, the reader feels at the end of the stanza, in the interest of a certain personification of the Soracte description that should convey something to the addressee. The identity, however, of the addressee remains unknown at this point, as does the nature of the relationship between the speaker and the addressee, aside from their relative ages. The physical location of the speaker and the addressee—aside from the fact that they may be somewhere near Soracte—and other matters mentioned above also remain unclear. And yet the last word of the stanza, *acuto* ("sharp"), points directly to the human observers of the scene, for it is they, not the rivers, that feel the sharpness of the cold.

The second stanza begins with a command to the addressee, *Dissolve frigus* . . . ("Dissolve the cold . . ."), and with particular instructions that show that speaker and addressee are at the fireside foretold by the earlier indications of a particular Alcaic model. For the reader, the imitation of Alcaeus recommences and indeed becomes closer than it was in the first stanza, to judge from the two surviving lines of the first stanza of Alcaeus. All of the second stanza of Alcaeus' poem (but no more) is preserved:

κάββαλλε τὸν χείμων', ἐπὶ μὲν τίθεις
πῦρ, ἐν δὲ κέρναις οἶνον ἀφειδέως
μέλιχρον, αὐτὰρ ἀμφὶ κόρσα
μάλθακον ἀμφι⟨βάλων⟩ γνόφαλλον

Overthrow the storm, laying on
fire, and mix wine unsparingly,
sweet (wine), while about your temples
you set a soft pillow [or a scarf].

This Alcaic stanza has four distinct elements: the opening injunction, the fire, the wine, and the pillow or scarf. Horace has preserved the first three, in the same sequence, and with *benignius* has even matched the line-final position and the scansion (ˉ ˉ ˘ ˉ) of "unsparingly" (ἀφειδέως). As in the first stanza, Horace coordinates his subject matter with the metrical sense units—injunction in the first, fire in the second, and wine in the third and fourth. The first two units are marked off by the coincidence of sense pause and caesura:

   1   2
dissolve frigus ◇ ‖ ligna super foco
             3
large reponens ◇ ‖ atque benignius
              4
deprome quadrimum Sabina
o Thaliarche, merum diota.

Horace's fuller prescription for the serving of the wine (units 3 and 4 in the scheme above) replaces Alcaeus' fourth element, the pillow or scarf. The reader's attention is thus drawn to this prescription. Why must the wine be Sabine and "four years old"? Sabine wine is ordinary, but does four years make it young or old? What is the "two-handled jar" (*diota*—a word of Greek origin that occurs nowhere else in Latin)?

A further variation worked by Horace on the Alcaic model is the introduction, in the vocative, of the name of the addressee, Thaliarchus. This Greek name, preceded by the interjection *o*, a Grecism, might stand for a particular Roman friend of Horace or for a type of person. The hiatus before the interjection (*Sabina,* / *o*) effectively stresses it and gives it an emotional intensity. "Thaliarchus" must be a particular person. The name means "Master of Revels" and is thus obviously related to the injunctions at the beginning of this stanza and in line 7—*deprome . . .* ("decant . . ."). The name itself seems to be part of the injunction: do as I say and be the master of revels that you ought to be. In any case, the interjection and the name, which are grander than the occasion calls for, seem somewhat facetious. For example, the reader has had no indication that more than two persons are present, whereas *thalia* in either the singular or the plural could suggest a group. Further, the name and the injunctions contribute to the impression already conveyed by the Alcaic sympotic model: the speaker is an older man, one who is going to give counsel, and Thaliarchus is a younger man, whose role (like that of Cyrnus in the Theognidea) is to imbibe good advice along with the wine.

The Greek elements in the second stanza are thus three. One is the imitation of Alcaeus, which belongs to the code operative exclusively between Horace and the reader. Another is the Greek word for the jar, *diota*. The third is the name Thaliarchus, preceded by the interjection *o*. The second and third elements belong both to the code operative between the speaker and Thaliarchus, a code to which the reader is privy, and to the one operative between Horace and the reader. The jar remains a problem for the reader. As part of the instructions, *diota* signified something obvious to Thaliarchus (note that it is the climactic word in the stanza), and yet the word, which occurs only here in Roman literature, is difficult for the reader to decode. The reader is well aware, however, that he is witnessing the Roman inscenation of a Greek social occasion, and the relation between the

Roman and the Greek strains is epitomized in the joining of the adjective *Sabina* to the Greek word *diota*. Does the Greekness of the occasion have anything to do with the fact that the speaker can give orders to his companion?

Like the second, the third stanza begins with an imperative. This time, however, the command is not practical but theoretical: "Leave everything else (that is, except our immediate need for warmth and wine) to the gods." Thaliarchus should do so because the gods are all-powerful; whether we want to or not, we have to entrust everything else to them; it is not worth our worrying about things completely outside our control. The speaker illustrates this point by conjuring up the picture of a storm on the ocean—the forces of nature at their most awesome—which the gods can calm when they will, and then the effects of the storm on the land, seen in the swaying of the trees, cease, too. This storm is thus described in terms of wind and the effects of wind, and it has nothing to do with the storm whose aftermath the speaker described in the still, frozen landscape of the first stanza. These battling winds of the third stanza are any storm. Did Horace have a Greek original for these winds (the Alcaic model is, to repeat, a fragment that ends with the stanza quoted above)? Is he describing a storm, or storms, that he has witnessed? These questions cannot be answered, and, even if they could, there would remain a perhaps more important consideration—that the speaker is describing an imaginary scene, one that he and Thaliarchus would not actually be able to see from the fireside even if a storm of this sort were blowing outside. The interior setting of the second stanza is thus framed by the aftermath of a storm (first stanza), to be visualized by Thaliarchus from indoors, and by a hypothetical hurricane (third stanza), to be imagined.

The versification itself of the third stanza represents the speaker's counsel in such a way that the gods and the storm, whose actions occupy the second and third units of the stanza, disappear abruptly, completely—and reassuringly. The effect of the sense pauses in the first and third lines is to isolate the storm on the ocean. This effect is emphasized by a variation on the rhythmic pattern of the third line

that was established in the first two stanzas, where a heavy word oc-
cupied the center of the line and the new unit began after the sixth
syllable. In the third stanza, a heavy, five-syllable word *begins* the third
line and completes the third sense unit and with it the description of
the storm. The fourth unit begins at the end of this word, after the
fifth syllable:

```
    1              2
permitte divis ‖ cetera,  ◊ qui simul
               3
stravere ventos ‖ aequore fervido
               4
deproeliantis,  ◊ nec cupressi
nec veteres agitantur orni.
```

The effect of cessation after the fifth syllable of the third line is intensified by the syntax. The relative pronoun *qui* in the first line refers to
the gods, who the reader expects will be the subject of the verb of
the relative clause that is interrupted by the temporal clause beginning with *simul:* "who, as soon as they have calmed the winds fighting
it out on the seething ocean, ..." But the relative pronoun and the
clause it introduces are abandoned, and a new sentence with new
subjects begins. The gods disappear. Further, the reader might have
expected this new sentence, despite the break in the syntax, to have
something to do with the ocean: for example, the new sentence
might have said, "the ocean is now serene." Instead, the new sentence shifts the scene to dry land, and cypresses and ashes are the
subjects.

These trees have different habitats. The deciduous ash, indig-
enous to Italy, grew on mountains.[7] The evergreen cypress, an im-
port, was an ornamental tree planted in chosen places.[8] (The funereal
uses of the cypress seem irrelevant to the context.) The ash and the
cypress are thus opposites—wild and domestic, "raw and cooked"—

7. Examples s.v. *ornus, -i* in OLD.
8. Second example in OLD s.v. *cupressus, -i.*

that embrace the whole range of earthly existence and thus are fitting images to sum up the first two stanzas—frozen nature outdoors, with its forests (*silvae*), and secure interior, heated by wood (*ligna*). The speaker tells Thaliarchus that, when the gods choose to end the storm, our whole environment, human and natural, is secure.

The ashes and cypresses are "old" (*veteres* applies to both). As the *silvae* of the first stanza were personified, so now are the ashes and cypresses. The personification is also conveyed by the verb *agitantur*, which, referring to human cares, means "to disturb" or "to trouble."[9] The old trees are no longer disturbed. Being old, they know enough not to care. The adjective "old" thus reinforces the reader's sense, deriving from the imitation of Alcaeus, that the speaker is older and Thaliarchus younger. The use of *veteres* implicitly gives the speaker's age as the authority for his advice. The reader can also now see how far Horace has departed from Alcaeus in his representation of the relationship between the speaker and the addressee. Nothing in the two surviving lines of Alcaeus' first stanza suggests personification of nature, and the reader suspects that the corresponding concern on the part of the speaker for the addressee's state of mind is also absent from Alcaeus. Whereas "Zeus" was the first word of Alcaeus' poem, the divine appears in Horace's only in the third stanza and then only as a realm so far beyond human competence that it should also be beyond human concern. Horace has reworked Alcaeus' first stanza in such a way as to show already at the opening of the poem the speaker's intention of instructing the addressee in his proper concerns. The personification of *silvae* and of ashes and cypresses in Horace's ode is a clue to the character of Thaliarchus and to the purpose of the speaker, whose advice will not be limited to the practical matters of stanza 2.

The first three stanzas began with a verb in the second person singular. The fourth breaks this pattern, beginning with an indirect question ("What will happen tomorrow"?). Then the pattern is resumed, for, in the first line of the stanza, the speaker addresses Thal-

---

9. Lewis and Short IIB and OLD 8b s.v. *agito, -are*.

iarchus in the imperative mood again: "Shun to ask." The command is grammatically positive but logically negative and is balanced by another command that is both grammatically and semantically positive: "count as gain any day that fortune will give you." The reader's sense of a change in the pattern is borne out, however, by the speaker's tone as it emerges from word order and meter. In each of the first three lines of the stanza, sense pauses and metrical pauses are disjointed:

1   2
quid sit futurum ‖ cras, ◊ fuge quaerere, et
                    3
quem fors dierum ‖ cumque dabit, ◊ lucro
adpone ◊

Cras, the first word of the second unit, goes with the indirect question of the first unit and is emphatically isolated in the first line between caesura and strong sense pause: "what will happen—tomorrow—shun to ask." (Compare the isolation of the temporal expression *nec iam* in the first stanza.) The speaker hastens to add another command, with *et* at the end of the line and elision of the final syllable of the word preceding *et*. (This is proof enough that Horace did not compose line by line.) The second command, beginning in the second line, is preceded by a relative clause parallel to the indirect question preceding the first command. This (approximate) syntactic parallelism between lines 1 and 2 is reinforced by the balanced pattern of words (monosyllable—monosyllable—trisyllable) initiating the first and second lines and even by the -um rhyme before the caesuras. The parallelism of sound is, in fact, elaborate:

qu- s- -rum ‖ c-
qu- -s -rum ‖ c-.

Further, the beginning of the third unit (*cumque dabit*, which is isolated not only by tmesis and the ensuing sense pause but also because it constitutes a choriamb) has to complete the relative clause, just as *cras*, in the second unit, completed the indirect question of the first.

The reader's sense of (a controlled) disjointedness continues in the third line, in which a strong sense pause occurs unexpectedly (after the first three stanzas) after the first word, *adpone*, the imperative that completes the sense of the preceding line.

Versification conveys the change in the speaker's attitude to Thaliarchus: it is part of the code by which Horace represents to the reader the relationship between the speaker and Thaliarchus. From *quaerere* (that is, asking unanswerable questions) the reader sees what the speaker objects to in Thaliarchus; from meter and word order, what the new (after the first three stanzas) emotional cast of the objection is. In the fourth stanza, the speaker for the first time directly challenges Thaliarchus' outlook. (Thaliarchus did not have to take *permitte divis cetera* as ad hominem; it could have seemed mere attitudinizing.) What Thaliarchus likes to do and probably considers admirably serious—namely, ponder the future—is dismissed, and what he probably scorns—accepting whatever the day may bring—is enjoined as the principle he should follow.

After the strong sense pause at the beginning of the third line (15), the speaker deploys a carrot and a stick to enforce his somewhat agitated, head-on exhortation. The carrot is the diversion of Thaliarchus' attention to love or loves (*amores* is not necessarily poetic plural) and to dancing, with the implication in *sperne* that Thaliarchus has really gone too far in his neglect of these activities. The stick is the reminder, in the word *puer* (which is predicative: "while you are young"), of the relationship between the two of them: the speaker has the authority of age. The speaker seems to present love(s) and dancing as two logically complementary components of the same concept, for example, the pleasures of youth:

4

◊ nec dulcis amores
sperne puer neque tu choreas.

The connection between *amores* and *choreas* is all the closer if *nec* is not a connective (the tone of the speaker as discerned in the first three units of the stanza would prompt the reader to feel that a new sentence is beginning) but a correlative with *neque*. Further, each of the nouns *amores* and *choreas* is trisyllabic, each is in line-final position, and they are metrically identical (˘ ˘). Horace has given them as much weight as possible (at this point the reader has no reason not to feel that the stanza is end-stopped, as the first three stanzas were). But, just because these two words have such weight and are so crucial to the speaker's argument, the reader begins to wonder if they are, in fact, simply complementary. If so, together they have a rhetorical amplitude that *amores*, for example, by itself would not have. But a merely rhetorical flourish of this sort would be inconsistent with the style of the ode as the reader has experienced it to this point. What are these dances (*choreas*)? Are they really in the same category as *amores*? Or are they two different, unrelated activities? At this point, the reader has no way to answer these questions. Again, like the *diota*, these words obviously communicated something from the speaker to Thaliarchus.

The fourth stanza is not end-stopped, however. Its final sentence carries over into the beginning of the fifth stanza in the form of a subordinate temporal clause. To his injunction, the speaker attaches a proviso: "as long as peevish, hoary age is removed from your green youth." The antithesis between youth and age, which became more and more explicit as the basis of the relationship between the speaker and Thaliarchus, is now expressed in terms of Thaliarchus' own life. The contrasting words for youth and age are juxtaposed on either side of the caesura:

donec <u>virenti</u> ‖ <u>canities</u> abest
morosa. ◊

Old age, which, as the basis of the speaker's authority, might have seemed an extrinsic consideration to Thaliarchus, now appears as intrinsic to his own life, as lying on the same continuum (*abest*) with his youth. The contrast of colors, green and grayish white, is not permanent; the former will become the latter. As *morosa*, old age has no share in the sweet loves and dances to which the speaker has called Thaliarchus.

After the somewhat abrupt full stop at the beginning of the second line (18), the speaker, in the same excited (or mock-peevish?) tone that emerged in the preceding stanza, exclaims, "Now the field (that is, the Campus Martius) and the open places (that is, of the town) and light whisperings at nightfall should be sought, at a prearranged hour":

3
◇ nunc et ‖ campus et areae
4
lenesque sub noctem susurri
conposita repetantur hora.

The different conjunctions that join the three things in the speaker's list (*et . . . et . . . -que*) have the effect of distinguishing the first two as separate entities and of suggesting that the third belongs with the second as a connected whole.[10] The open spaces of the city are where Thaliarchus will hear light whisperings—presumably from the lips of a girl, but the places conjured up by the speaker are still unpopulated. The three items, field, open spaces, and whisperings, thus reduce to two, and these two seem to be the venues for the two activities named in the preceding stanza, love and dancing—the field for dancing and the open spaces for love. The emphasis on place is matched by an emphasis on time, or, rather, on the time of day, dusk, and on the appointed time at which a meeting can take place. The time scale of the preceding stanza (*quid sit futurum, quem fors dierum cumque dabit*) is scaled down to dimensions within human competence.

The sixth and final stanza begins with anaphora of the phrase *nunc et* from the preceding stanza. Within the anaphora, however, there is variation, since *et* is now not a connective but an adverb, "also." This final stanza is without a finite verb, which is understood from the last line of the preceding stanza (*repetantur*). The absence both of a verb and, curiously, of personal agents has the effect of freezing the action. Thaliarchus has been invited to imagine himself in this

10. OLD s.v. -que 1b, 6a, 9b, 10a.

scene, but this is the only stanza in which he is not directly addressed (though direct address already begins to fade, with virenti—sc. tibi— in the penultimate stanza). And what the speaker has in mind is not Thaliarchus but the girl, her laugh, her arm, her finger. What began as an exclamation (18) now modulates to a calmer mood. The speaker's fascination with the scene suggests that it is as much a memory from his own past as a hope for Thaliarchus' present or future.

The speaker builds up the picture as slowly as possible. The first line has the glimmer of sense:

nunc et latentis ‖ proditor intumo.

"Betrayer of the hiding . . . ," but who or what is the betrayer, who or what is hiding? And intumo awaits a noun or pronoun. The second line gradually completes the sense (in the following, capital letters stand above nouns, lower-case letters stand above adjectives or participles, and a noun in apposition to another noun is indicated by a superscript number):

```
        a        B      c
nunc et latentis ‖ proditor intumo
   b    A     B¹       C
gratus puellae ‖ risus ab angulo.
```

At the beginning of the second line, proditor finds an adjective and latentis finds a noun. The "betrayer" is "welcome," and the "hiding" one is a girl. The arrangement of the four words in question is chiastic:

```
a       B
    ×
b       A.
```

The two opening words of the chiasmus (aB) are placed on either side of the caesura, whereas the two closing words (bA) are before the caesura; thus they seem climactic, giving promise of completing the sense. And yet "the welcome betrayer" remains unspecified. The sense is completed only by the word beyond the caesura in the second line. The betrayer of the girl turns out to be her own laugh, which is what is now welcome, as the adjective *gratus* is reoriented in a new pattern. The suspension created by the chiasmus is thus resolved by the emergence of this other, interlocking pattern that incorporates three elements from the chiasmus:

a ‖ B
A ‖ B¹.

The two pairs of words (*latentis proditor, puellae risus*) are arranged symmetrically on either side of the caesuras. Finally, the sense of *intumo* is completed by the prepositional phrase (*ab angulo*) at the end of the second line: "from the depth of her hiding place." The description of the scene is now also completed with the location of the girl, or, more precisely, of her laugh. The rhyming and the rhythmic equivalence of the two components of the phrase (*intumo . . . angulo*) are a climactic coupling of two lines already densely interlaced. At the same time, the word order itself of the phrase reinforces the sense of the lines.

The laugh, voluntarily betraying her location, is not all that Thaliarchus has to hope for. He will also snatch a pledge from her, a shoulder bracelet or a ring from her finger, which will only feign resistance. The word order of each of the two concluding lines is simple—a noun and a participle (Dd), followed by two nouns (EF) (in the ablative or dative) depending on the participle (d):

D   d   4 E
pignusque dereptum lacerto
     F   f
aut digito male pertinaci.

The words make sense as they come. E and Ff, governed by d, are grouped in the fourth unit of the stanza. The organization of the two concluding lines could not be clearer. The clarity and openness of these lines serve to resolve the density of the first two lines, and the effect is one of release, just as the girl releases the ring from her finger. The last two words of the stanza and of the poem, *male pertinaci* ("feebly resisting"), also recapitulate the self-betrayal of the first part of the stanza. The ring is an alternative to the arm bracelet. *Aut* implies: "if not that, then . . ."[11] Thus the speaker concludes by intensifying the feeling of promise in the scene he has conjured up for Thaliarchus. The youth will certainly get one pledge or the other, and accordingly he will certainly get that which is pledged.

The last stanza is climactic in the relationship between the speaker and Thaliarchus in that the speaker has now completely subverted the authority, age, that was the basis of his advice, and he has released Thaliarchus into his youth. It was the very peevishness of age, perhaps, or the jocular pretense of peevishness, that pushed the speaker to this extreme. Thaliarchus and the speaker part ways. This change in the relationship has transpired within a single setting, by the fireside, on a winter's day. What has happened to Horace's and the reader's relationship? Although the Alcaic model (338 Lobel-Page) is the main component of the code of communication, this model is preserved only to the extent that the sympotic setting, given in the second stanza, is preserved to the end. At the fourth stanza, perhaps already at the third, the reader becomes aware of a departure from Alcaeus in the direction of specifically Roman concerns. Thaliarchus is a Roman youth. The speaker's advice (stanzas 4–6) looks to Roman places and activities. Horace and Alcaeus part ways, too.

The Alcaic stanza, however, as distinguished from the particular model (338 Lobel-Page), necessarily persists to the end, and, for the reader, the principal means of achieving closure is through Horace's shaping of the stanza's potential into the climax of technique displayed in the first two lines of stanza 6. Thus, even within his necessary adherence to the Alcaic stanza, Horace can free himself from Alcaeus by surpassing him. As a poetic feat, these lines are a confirmation to the reader of the possibility of release from care that the speaker of the poem has affirmed at the ethical level. In effect, the reader experiences and accepts the triumph of Horace as the success of the speaker's exhortation to Thaliarchus. The convergence of the two relationships is climactic.

11. OLD s.v. *aut* 1a, 2a, 3.

2

. . . .

Second
Reading

The second reading returns from the end of the poem to the beginning and seeks an interpretation within the horizon established by the first reading. The second therefore in no way replaces the first. On the contrary, the second looks to questions posed by the first and to "significance still left open," "still unfulfilled significance."[1] The hypothesis of the second reading is that the poem will present itself as a whole to interpretation as it did to an aesthetic, perceptual reading. In the main, the second is a reflective rereading of a sort familiar to almost anyone who reads lyric poetry, albeit a rereading controlled by the premise of the aesthetic character of the text as the basis of interpretation. At the same time, the reader does not intend an "objective," totalizing interpretation but assumes the partiality of his perspective. This assumption will open the way to the third, historical reading, which tries to establish the original audience's "horizon of expectation,"[2] and to the history of the poem's reception, against the alterity of which the reader can measure his own reading.

The first reading discovered an aesthetic unity in the deploy-

1. Jauss 1982, 141, 145.

2. This expression was coined by Jauss. For references to its first occurrences see Jauss 1982, 200 n. 11. But Holub (1984, 59) states that Karl Popper and Karl Mannheim had used the expression "long before Jauss."

ment of two codes, one between the speaker and Thaliarchus, the other between Horace and the reader. The first of these codes established a relationship between an older and a younger man, and this dramatic situation, changing in mood in the course of the poem, is the most palpable of the poem's unities, founded as it is on a strict unity of place: they sit by the fireside as the older man dispenses advice to the younger. But if that relationship establishes the unity of the poem, what, besides the difference in their ages and their assumed friendship, constitutes that relationship? From the first stanza, questions arose. The winter scene of that stanza was to some degree personified and in this respect should have communicated something to Thaliarchus and something to the reader about Thaliarchus. The personification of the landscape should have shown something about the speaker's attitude toward Thaliarchus. The significance of Soracte, then, remains a question. The poem is often called "The Soracte Ode" in response to the prominence of the visual image of the mountain. Likewise, the speaker's explicit "theoretical" advice, from the beginning of the third stanza on, should tell the reader something about the dramatic relationship between the speaker and Thaliarchus, about the personality of Thaliarchus as perceived by the speaker. A closely related question concerns the name Thaliarchus. If it is a playful pseudonym for a person or a type, as it seems to be, does it have significance beyond the second stanza, in which it appears to be related to the demand for more wine? Why does the speaker give orders to Thaliarchus?

In pursuing the answers to such questions concerning a poem written two thousand years ago, the reader inevitably departs slightly from Jauss's method. The reader's own reflections will not be sufficient but will be supported by historical and philological research. Even Jauss relied on research for his interpretive second reading of Baudelaire's "Spleen." Jauss, however, could find help in Baudelaire's Fusées and Mon coeur mis à nu, and, combining passages from these works with psychoanalytic theory, he produced a "biographic-psychological excursus."[3] Though many of Horace's poems are un-

3. Jauss 1982, 167.

doubtedly autobiographical in certain respects, the information they contain is mediated through poetry and cannot be formed into a commentary on the problems the reader faces in interpreting the poem under discussion here. Nevertheless, the other poems of Horace and, for that matter, the poems of other Latin poets are necessary sources for semantics, usage, and other matters in *C.* 1.9.

If, however, the second reading requires historical and philological information of this sort, how does it differ from the third reading, which attempts to recover the original audience's response to the poem? The answer to this question lies in the relation of the three readings to one another. The research that attends the second reading does not originate in a historical perspective on the poem but in the interpretive questions prompted by the first reading. Thus the historical and philological aspects of the second reading are controlled by the aesthetic perspective of the first one, and different readers at different times will, in a second reading following Jauss's method, apply the traditional methods of classical scholarship to different places in the poem in accordance with their first readings. The third reading, on the other hand, aims to be strictly historical in focus and should provide the reader with a means of gauging the change from the original audience's horizon to his own.

Vides ut . . . ? "Do you see how . . . ?" And the most prominent thing you see is Soracte. What did the speaker expect Thaliarchus to see in Soracte? An answer that can be ruled out immediately is natural beauty. The Romans "seem to have continued throughout their history insensible to the attractions of mountain scenery."[4] Roman writers describe mountains as "inhospitable," "remote," "cold," "frightful," "horrid," "bristling," and "shaggy."[5] Mountains were not the locales of pleasant activities. The Romans did not have the L.L. Bean catalog from which to order winter clothing, and they did not

---

4. Hyde 1915, 78. For a fuller statement of the matter see Friedlaender 1922, 480–85, beginning at the marginal heading "Kein Verständnis für die Schönheit der Gebirgnatur."

5. See Hyde 1915, 78–79 and 79 n. 1 for references.

practice skating, skiing, and tobogganing. Nor were they mountain climbers.[6] When, apropos of Hannibal's difficulties in crossing the Apennines, Livy refers to similar, earlier difficulties with the succinct phrase *Alpium foeditatem* (21.58.3), he seems to refer not simply to bad weather but to a general foulness.

Did Soracte, however, have particular associations that would fit with the rest of the winter scene, somewhat personified by the distress of the bending branches? Though Soracte was an important source of limestone (Vitruvius 2.7), the answer to the reader's question concerning Horace's poem lies in the mountain's cultic identity or identities. Its name is Faliscan. It was sacred to the Di Manes and was the site of the worship of Dis Pater, who was called Soranus, a Sabine word. The servants of the god were called Hirpi, from the Sabine word for wolf (Servius on *Aen.* 11.785). Later, this underworld god was somehow identified with Apollo, and the Hirpi were known for the rite in his honor in which they walked barefoot over burning coals (Verg. *Aen.* 11.785–90; Pliny NH 7.2.11; Sil. It. 5.175ff.). The etiological story concerning the origin of the name Hirpi includes mention of poisonous exhalations from caves on Soracte (Servius ibid.; cf. Pliny NH 2.95[93].2). Birds that breathed them fell from the air dead. On Soracte there was also a poisonous spring, and again birds are mentioned as the victims (Pliny NH 31.19.2). Wild goats leapt sixty feet and more from Soracte's crags (Cato Hist. 52 Peter = 2.16 Jordan). Two funerary inscriptions from Falerii Novi, near Soracte, show that a certain family had a hereditary augurship related to the mountain and its cult(s). One of these inscriptions has the word *harispex* (CIL 11.3158, p. 476 = 60 Deecke), the other the Faliscan *haracna* (Lat. *haruspex*; CIL 11.3159, p. 476 = 61 Deecke); both of these words have in apposition the noun *sorex* (≠ Lat. *sorex* "shrew-mouse"; = Lat. *Soractinus*; cf. *sancti custos Soractis Apollo* at Verg. *Aen.* 11.785 and *mons Sorax* in Porphyrion on Hor. C. 1.9.1–2).

Soracte was a strange place. Enlightened Romans did not take its cults and augurs very seriously. A remark reported in Cicero's *De*

6. With the occasional exception of Aetna: see Friedlaender 1922, 485.

divinatione illustrates their attitude. In this dialogue between Cicero and his brother Quintus, the latter undertakes to defend divination against the former. Under the heading of augurs, Quintus uses the example of the augur Appius Claudius, who, in Cicero's consulship, predicted the Catilinarian conspiracy. And yet, says Quintus, "your [augural] colleagues used to laugh at him and say now that he was a Pisidian, now that he was a Soran augur, since they thought that there was no presentiment and no knowledge of what would really happen in the future" (1.47).[7] With Quintus' use of "Soran," compare Soran (*Soranus*) as an epithet of the Dis Pater worshipped on Soracte. A "Soran augur" was a joke—in the same class with oriental superstition. In short, the Faliscan-named mountain and its religious practices were distinctly non-Roman. In the *Aeneid*, it is an Etruscan, the ignoble Arruns, who describes the rite of the Hirpi in his prayer to Apollo just before he spears Camilla.

In the ode, Soracte is, both to the reader and to Thaliarchus, not just a prominent example of wintry coldness (though coldness by itself was bad enough) but something more profoundly antipathetic. To dissolve the cold is not only to escape the cares intimated in the scene; it is also to distance oneself from that which is alien, to return to one's own. Even if the speaker and Thaliarchus are somewhere in the countryside outside of Rome, they are Romans in relation to Soracte and the frozen landscape. The first stanza and the third bear the same relation to the second: what is outside should be left outside; what is inside is our appropriate concern. The explicit

7. Pease (1920, 288–89) points out that Cicero was not an augur and thus did not have augurs as colleagues until 53 B.C. Quintus thus refers to remarks heard after 53 B.C. and probably before the death of Appius Claudius in 47 B.C.

In *De Div.* 1.1 the Pisidians are grouped with the Cilicians and Pamphylians as believers in the flight and song of birds as infallible signs of the future.

Pease (1920, 289) takes *Soranum* as a reference not to Soracte but to the town Sora. He has no real evidence. As augurs are under discussion, and as there were hereditary augurs who had the epithet Sorex, it seems more reasonable to take the remark reported by Quintus as referring to them (for the form *Soranus* that Quintus uses, cf. Dis Soranus).

return to Rome, in the form of the advice in stanzas 4 to 6, is thus already implicit in stanzas 1 to 3. The image of Soracte initiates the theme of the alien—the *cetera*, the unknowable future. If the mountain suggested the local *haruspices*, it is an even more suitable way for the speaker to indicate that from which Thaliarchus should sequester himself.

Soracte is also absent in two other senses. First, with *dissolve frigus*, the reader receives confirmation that speaker and addressee have been indoors from the beginning. Now the generality of the description, especially the plural *flumina*, makes sense. If speaker and addressee had been outdoors, how many rivers could they have seen from one place?[8] How likely is it that Horace represented the pair strolling through the countryside? Would the Alcaeus model have changed scene from the first stanza to the second? There is a gap, to be sure, between the first and second stanzas in C. 1.9, but it is precisely this gap that causes the reader to form a connection, to find the location of the speaker of the first stanza, to re-create a "virtual dimension" of the text.[9] This dimension, impervious to an approach that demands that the text "be left in its silences" and that will only comment on the words that are there in the text, emerges in the process of reading, as the text is realized by a reader.[10]

Second, since Thaliarchus would not have been able to look out a window, what he sees he sees in his mind's eye, and this mental operation presupposes and requires the absence of that which is visualized. What Gilbert Ryle says of Mount Helvellyn holds for Thaliarchus' view of Soracte:

> Seeing Helvellyn in one's mind's eye does not entail, what seeing Helvellyn and seeing snapshots of Helvellyn entail, the having of visual sensations. It does involve the thought of having a view of Helvellyn and it is therefore a more sophisticated op-

8. Good remarks on the rivers appear in Gelsomino 1962, 564–65.

9. See Iser 1980, 54–55, for the phrase "virtual dimension," and 58–64 on the establishment of consistency in the process of reading.

10. Iser 1980, 50.

eration than that of having a view of Helvellyn. It is one utilization among others of the knowledge of how Helvellyn should look, or, in one sense of the verb, it is thinking how it should look. The expectations which are fulfilled in the recognition at the sight of Helvellyn are not indeed fulfilled in picturing it, but the picturing of it is something like a rehearsal of getting them fulfilled. So far from picturing involving the having of faint sensations, or wraiths of sensations, it involves missing just what one would be due to get, if one were seeing the mountain.[11]

To picture or visualize the mountain is thus at the same to experience its absence. The speaker's *Vides* paradoxically inculcates in Thaliarchus a sense of the remoteness of Soracte. *Vides* is thus of a piece with the injunction, *permitte divis cetera*. The "real" winter landscape outdoors is as remote from the fireside by which the speaker and Thaliarchus sit as is the hypothetical storm at sea to be described in the third stanza.[12]

The generality of *flumina*, noticed above, is one example of "missing just what one would be due to get" if one were looking at Soracte. The ambiguity of *alta* in the phrase *alta . . . nive* is another.[13] The snow may be "deep" or "high," that is, high on Soracte, but Thaliarchus hardly needs to decide, for the speaker's summons to a picturing of Soracte is a deliberate summons to a kind of thinking ("a more sophisticated operation") that replaces the physical perception of the object. The reader's experience is something like Thaliarchus'.

11. Ryle 1949, 270, quoted in Iser 1980, 57.

12. Cf. Williams 1968, 635–36, who speaks of an attitude that "deterred Roman poets from finding inspiration in looking at the world with their own eyes and persuaded them to interpose between their own vision and the real world the already existing descriptions of earlier writers. In Horace, *Odes* i.9 the opening words *vides ut . . .* suggest an immediate visual effect but the details which follow are conceptual, not only are they mainly taken from Alcaeus, but the words *laborantes* and *constiterint* explore a non-visual level whose interest lies in the application to nature of terms that apply to human behavior."

13. Nisbet and Hubbard 1970 ad loc.; Clay 1989.

The banal phrase *alta . . . nive*—any snow worth mentioning in Latin literature is usually either melting or deep[14]—at first seems to be linked to *stet*, but then the reader must readjust his (mental) perception and associate the phrase with *candidum*. The phrase moves kaleidoscopically from one place in the sentence to another and loses its banality in a *callida iunctura*, a skillful collocation of words of the sort that Horace called for in the *Ars Poetica* (46–48). The reader experiences a mental revision corresponding to Thaliarchus' visual recollection of the scene outdoors.

The command *dissolve frigus* at the beginning of the second stanza is thus a command to complete the detachment that has already been established: the verb *dissolvere* can mean "to break one's connection to."[15] To "dissolve the cold" indoors is to remove the only link between indoors and outdoors. Having established one kind of inwardness, the speaker, in the rest of the poem, will also inculcate another. The series of imperatives beginning with *permitte* at the beginning of stanza 3 all require mental activities of Thaliarchus—reflection and imagination. Picturing Soracte was the first and easiest lesson.

To recapitulate, in the transition from stanza 1 to stanza 2, the first claim on the reader's attention was the uncertainty of the location of the speaker and the addressee. He could not completely imagine that location until the beginning of the second stanza, although the Alcaic model provided a hint. The reader and Thaliarchus were thus involved in parallel imaginative processes. The reader, in his realization of a "virtual dimension" of the poem, came to imagine an indoor setting for everything he had read from the beginning of the poem. Thaliarchus, for his part, through the visualizations required

---

14. Deep: Lucr. 6.963–64; Caes. Gal. 7.8.2; Hor. *Epod.* 6.7; S. 1.2.105–6 (after Callimachus); Livy 43.18.2, 43.21.7; Plin. NH 5.15.1; Tac. *Hist.* 1.79.8. Cf. Verg. G. 3.354–55: *aggeribus niveis informis et alto / terra gelu.* On the relation of Horace's deep snow and frozen rivers to Verg. G. 1.310 (*cum nix alta iacet, glaciem cum flumina trudunt*), see the suggestive remarks of Gelsomino (1962, 553–57).

15. OLD s.v. 3.

of him in stanzas 1 and 3, experiences the remoteness and alterity of everything outside the warm room in which he sits or reclines with his older friend.

It is a country house, as *ligna* (5) shows. "Four-year-old" wine points in the same direction. The "Sabine jar" is an amphora of local fabric. "Sabine" is not an epithet transferred from the wine to the jar but applies to both the jar and the wine.[16] The native jar has a Greek name, *diota*, which, though unattested elsewhere in Latin, cannot be a nonce word. Its morphology presupposes an earlier life in the language: it has been given a feminine ending (δίωτος, -ον is an adjective of two endings) and is used as a substantive. The word belongs to the group of substantivized adjectives in the vocabularies of particular groups and activities.[17] It will be one of those Grecisms that came into Latin through trade contacts and will have been an everyday word of a kind that Horace likes to use in the *Odes*.[18] Meaning "two-eared," it would have referred to a two-handled jar, to repeat, an amphora, as δίωτος does in Greek. It is a storage jar, as *deprome* (cf. C. 1.37.5–6)

16. Country house: Rudd 1960, 392, against Bagnani 1954; West 1967, 5–6.

"Four-year-old" wine: Gow 1952, 2:167, on Theoc. *Id.* 7.147: "No doubt for simple folk or al fresco entertainments four-year-old wine, whether Greek or Roman, counted as old, though connoisseurs might not have approved it." On Sabine wine see Tchernia 1986, 207, 274, 344.

"Sabine jar": Archaeology has not revealed any example of a Sabine jar, but the proven existence of numerous pottery ateliers throughout Italy (see the survey of Tchernia 1986) makes local fabric extremely likely. Consider also the likelihood that wine was shipped from the Sabine territory to Rome (Tchernia 1986, 178). Cf. the curious note of Orelli (1886) on *Sabina*: "Alii *Sabina* minus recte interpretantur de vase tantummodo fictili, qualia ex ea regione Romam advehi solita sint." One wonders who these *alii* were and what their evidence was.

"Sabine" applies to both jar and wine: Kiessling and Heinze 1917; Numberger 1972 ad loc.

17. Hofmann 1965, 154–55.

18. Hofmann 1965, 759ff. Axelson 1945, in chap. 4 ("Zur Wortwahl des Odendichters Horaz"), gives a list of prosaic words.

shows.[19] If the addressee is going to play the thaliarch or symposiarch, then the speaker playfully encourages him by giving the native jar a Greek name. (This is the one point at which the two codes of communication may converge, because here the "Greekness" of the occasion becomes something that the speaker is communicating, albeit ironically, to Thaliarchus.) The notion of four (quadrimum) from two (diota) is also playful. Was Thaliarchus, anxious about the future (stanza 4), one of those who went in for the Babylonian numeri (cf. C. 1.11.1–3)? If so, let him concentrate instead on this alternative mathematics. (As thaliarch, he would also have to determine the ratio of wine to water.)

Though in the first reading the name Thaliarchus seemed to be specifically related to the injunction deprome, and so forth, the associations of its first element, thal-, are more elaborate. To be sure, they include feasting (to which the adjective thaleia always applies in archaic epic), wine (along with thalia or thaliai in Xen. 1.12 West, where a symposium is about to take place; Ion of Chios 26.3 West; Stesich. 148.8 Page Supplementum), and pleasure (Archil. 11.2 West; Theog. 983–4 West; Stesich. ibid.). They extend, however, beyond the sympotic setting to take in song and dance (Ion of Chios 26.11 West; Theog. 778 West; Hom. H. Merc. 454; cf. molpē at Xen. ibid.). The name Thaliarchus thus already includes the notion that the speaker makes explicit in choreas (16). Another association is youth (Theog. 983–88 West; H. Merc. ibid.; Bacchyl. 3.89; cf. trag. adesp. 327 Nauck; consider also the Homeric θαλερός).[20] The name Thaliarchus itself thus entails the opposition of youth to age that informs the poem. The first element of the name is the base of the verb thallein—"to sprout, grow" of trees and metaphorically "to thrive, flourish" of persons. The speaker uses a parallel metaphor in Latin in virenti (tibi), and in a nodal context in which the speaker stresses the youth of Thaliarchus and

---

19. Weise 1882, 73. As E. L. Will has written to me, this jar would be Form 1 in H. Dressel's typology of Roman amphoras in CIL XV.2, plate II.

20. Some good remarks on the name Thaliarchus appear in Cupaiuolo (1965, 280–81), for whom youth is the point of the name.

mentions all of its possibilities. In the following quotation of that context, the nodal features are underlined:

> nec dulcis amores
> sperne puer neque tu choreas
>
> donec virenti canities abest
> morosa. nunc et campus et areae
> (15–18)

The youth of Thaliarchus and the opposition of youth to age are the starkest points. The other nodal features are more difficult. The word order of lines 15–16 (object-verb-subject, subject-[sc. verb]-object) seems to give equal weight to the two objects, *amores* and *choreas*, and the postponement of the subject *tu* in such a way that it is juxtaposed with *choreas* might suggest—the suggestion was already there in the name Thaliarchus—that dancing is essential to the fulfillment of his youth.[21] Marcus Caelius Rufus, one of the most conspicuous young men around town in the generation before "Thaliarchus," was noted for his skill in dancing.[22] Further, the parallelism of *campus et areae* seems to reinforce that of *amores* and *choreas*, and, as appeared in the first reading, the speaker seems to name, and to distinguish between, the venues appropriate to love and dancing. The Campus Martius was a place not only for physical training but also for fun.[23]

---

21. On the position of *tu* see Nutting (1933), who argues that the pronoun is hardly more than a "rhetorical flourish." C. K. (*sic*) replies to him in note 11 of the same article that "it is emphatic . . . , and that it applies with equal emphasis to the two clauses."

22. Macr. 3.14.15, for whom it was not a laudatory attainment.

23. Cic. *pro Caelio* 11: *exercitatione et ludo campestri*; cf. Hor. *Sat.* 1.6.26. In *pro Mur.* 13 Cicero defends Murena against the charge of dancing. Murena could not have been a dancer unless he also indulged in certain other activities. He did not indulge in those activities. Therefore he was not a dancer. *Tempestivi convivi, amoeni loci, multarum deliciarum comes est extrema saltatio.* These three circumstances of dancing could represent three distinct venues. An *amoenus locus* was to be found in the gardens and groves of the Campus Martius (Strabo 5.236). You

The node is completely dissolved, however. After line 18, the reader hears no more of youth and age, dancing is forgotten, and love is to the fore. The one thing, love, in the nodal context that is not suggested by the first element of the name Thaliarchus, proves to be the focus of the speaker's advice to Thaliarchus. Horace misdirects the reader, but in such a way that, in reorienting himself, the reader discovers, to his satisfaction and amusement, what the speaker's agenda really was. The reader can recover his sense of the poem's direction because of the change of tone that appeared in the first reading. With *nunc et campus et areae*, the reader knows that the speaker's own preoccupations have taken over.

The change of tone, which began in the first line of stanza 4, results in an overturning of the apparent hierarchy age-youth that was given in the Alcaic model and founded the advice of the older speaker to the younger Thaliarchus. Youth is now superior to age. This reversal emerges from the two commonplaces with which the fourth stanza begins: don't worry about the future; count each new day as gain. The second commonplace is Epicurean and also proverbial.[24] *Lucrum*, however, the ode's only explicit metaphor, looks to a sphere, bookkeeping or accounting, to which nothing else in the ode is related. Despite its proverbial character, this metaphoric use of *lucrum* gives the reader pause. "Count each new day as gain" is not really a confirmation of "Don't worry about the future." First, this gain can be tallied only as the present opens into the future. Whatever fortune "will give" (*dabit*: future tense) amounts, from the perspective of Thaliarchus and the speaker, to a past achieved in the future, to what might be called a future past. Second, because this future is in the life of a person, Thaliarchus, the accumulation of days is a loss as much as a gain: he grows older, losing his youth, in order to calculate his gain.

---

might encounter a Cynthia strolling in the portico of Pompey in the Campus Martius: Prop. 1.32.11–12; cf. Ovid *Ars* 1.67.

24. Pl. *Mer.* 553–54: *id iam lucrumst / quod vivis.* Ter. *Phorm.* 251: *quidquid praeter spem eveniet, omne id deputabo esse in lucro.* Ov. *Tr.* 1.3.68: *in lucro est quae datur hora mihi.* Cic. *Fam.* 9.17.1: *de lucro prope iam quadriennium vivimus.*

The contradiction here between the metaphor, *lucrum*, and the speaker's intended advice in the fourth stanza ("Forget about the future and live in the present") is enacted in the speaker's substantiation of his advice in stanzas 5 and 6, beginning with *nunc* (18), the temporal adverb, "now," referring to Thaliarchus' time of life. The reader's response to lines 18–24 can best be described with reference to some general considerations concerning the representation of time. In *Critique of Pure Reason*, Kant wrote: "Time is nothing but the form of inner sense, that is, of the intuition of ourselves and of our inner state. . . . And just because this inner intuition yields no shape, we endeavor to make up for this want by analogies."[25] And the analogies of time are spatial. (Kant's favorite analogy of time is the line.) But the construction of any spatial analogue of time also itself belongs to time, and thus arises the philosophical problem of how the author of the analogical representation of time can include the time of the representation.

In the ode under discussion Horace engages this problem in his own fashion. Note, to begin with, the juxtaposition of the temporal adverb *nunc* and the designations of space, *et campus et areae*. The "now" to which the speaker exhorts Thaliarchus is immediately expressed in terms of places and spaces. These are analogues in the sense that they are the spaces appropriately corresponding to Thaliarchus' time of life, his youth, which is now, as represented by the speaker. The seasonal time of the places *represented* is spring or summer. The now of the *representation* itself, however, is winter, and the now of the representer is age as opposed to youth. But how, to restate the philosophical problem in terms of this poem, can the very time in which the speaker gives advice to Thaliarchus, the time of the poem, in which they sit by the fireside, enter into the time represented to Thaliarchus? How can now (the time of the poem) be now (the youth of Thaliarchus)? The reader interpreting the poem within the horizon of the first reading knows that the speaker's mood has

25. Kant 1929, B50. This passage is one of the epigraphs in Tiles 1989, which analyzes the philosophical difficulties of Kant's preferred analogue, the line.

changed at line 18 with the sentence beginning *nunc*. *As he speaks*, the speaker begins to recall his own youth. The advice he is giving becomes also a recollection. The speaker's past comes into the present in the mode of recollection. As the advice becomes a recollection, the present past time of the representation enters into the time represented in the advice. The now of the advice, the now that is recommended to Thaliarchus, is informed by a now of the advising, by the emergence into the present of the speaker's past.

The "future past" that is the reality of the present time recommended to Thaliarchus—as the metaphor of *lucrum* showed—is thus represented as the present past of the speaker. In the mode of recollection, a future past becomes a present past. Though the speaker could not directly represent the present as the present in his explicit advice in lines 13–18, in this meeting of Thaliarchus' future and the speaker's past in the outdoor spaces in lines 18–24, the present can be represented as present.

Within the explicit advice of lines 18–24, further, the reader encounters the same contradiction that was lurking in *lucrum*. On the one hand, as the first reading showed, the scene is oddly motionless. There is a girl's laugh, but it is like the photograph of a girl laughing. There is playful resistance; something is snatched. Again, it is like a photograph. Time is arrested. *Nunc* (21) is as pure as possible. On the other hand, the *pignus* that Thaliarchus should snatch is by definition a pledge for the future. The *nunc* to which Thaliarchus should devote himself includes and requires the future. *Sub noctem* and *composita . . . hora*, times within a day, presuppose that day and its passage. The girl's laugh is momentary, but it is a moment in time. The whole scene is set in spring or summer, and thus, as a possible *nunc* for Thaliarchus, who hears this advice during winter, it lies in the future. In sum, within the speaker's insistence on now, as opposed to concern with the future, even within the spatial images of this proposed now, time is set in motion. The future opens up.

At the end of the ode, the reader has the sense that the two components of the new hierarchy established in the fourth stanza (youth over age) are both contained in one of them, youth. As the past is an element in the future—as the metaphor *lucrum* revealed—age is an element in youth. Green is not the opposite of gray but is not yet gray; gray is not the opposite of green but is no longer green. The odd metrical emphasis on "no longer" (*nec iam*) in the second line of the ode finally makes sense: what is (like the winter landscape) is relative to what was (and what will be). And the turn in the poem that begins at line 13 becomes more comprehensible: the speaker's age was already an element in Thaliarchus' youth. Though friendship and the sympotic setting were the necessary condition of the speaker's advice, the advice reveals a deeper, temporal complicity between the pair, in which the older man does not have to envy the younger and the younger does not have to pity the older. For at line 13, the speaker can recover his youth not through mere nostalgia but through his younger friend Thaliarchus, in the sense that his past becomes the substance of his advice concerning Thaliarchus' present or future past. What they share is the past, even if the two pasts are separate on an absolute chronology. The poem relativizes that chronology in a process already adumbrated in the speaker's evocation of a winter landscape in stanza 1, in which "no longer" (2) put the description in relation to a prior state, and in his evocation of the storm at sea, in which "as soon as" (9) put the description in relation to a future state.

The reader can now reinterpret the hierarchies of stanzas 1 through 3 (inside-outside, warmth-cold, pleasure-pain, human-*cetera*, calm-storm). The inferior term was already included in the superior one. The terms of what the speaker had to—given the deontic model—present as hierarchical opposites lose their independent, opposed status as "no longer" and "as soon as" pervade them. Again, it is the speaker's dramatization of his advice, as distinguished from, say, a prose summary of this advice, that conveys the precariousness of the hierarchies. For vast change is what the speaker calls upon Thaliarchus to witness in his mind's eye—the stillness of nature *after* a snowstorm (stanza 1), the calmness of the earth *after* a hurricane (stanza 3). Thaliarchus was called upon to produce a *change* in his environment (stanza 2). The vast natural processes underlie and relativize the opposites in which the speaker seems to cast his advice. What is outside, *frigus*, is also inside; its force is relative to the warmth of the fire. Within the apparent stability and security of the fireside setting, change is already at work. What presents itself as change in the first three stanzas then presents itself as time in the last three.[26]

The poem ends with the speaker's memories cast in the form of advice concerning Thaliarchus' present time, in which the unfolding of the future is almost explicitly foreseen. This advice begins with certain spatial settings, and, as at various points earlier in the ode, Thaliarchus is in effect called upon to visualize what the speaker describes. These two processes, the speaker's remembering and Thaliarchus' visualizing, are related. (Ryle discusses memory and visualizing, or picturing, under the same heading, imagination.)[27] The two activities share various traits. In the ode, what Thaliarchus is asked to visualize is something that he has very recently seen and can remember. (In stanza 3, he is asked to use his imagination in a somewhat different way to visualize a hurricane at sea.) For Thaliarchus, then, the poem begins and ends in the same mode, that of imagination. Not only is he in the same place, at the fireside, but also he is in the same state of mind throughout. The speaker, in his avuncular, sententious style, would at first (stanzas 1 to 3) have seemed to be detached from this imaginative mode, except that his personifications of the trees (stanzas 1 and 3) revealed his own way of visualizing them. He was, then, not simply calling upon Thaliarchus to visualize them; he was also picturing them himself in his own fashion. The speaker,

26. A reading very close to my second reading is that of Segal (1981), who states: "The arbitrariness of the poem's frame cuts off continuity at both extremes and gives us a discontinuity which is unnatural and false to experience. But that very unnaturalness, that deliberate distortion of reality, is a potent element in the 'meaning' of the poem. The silence which frames its beginning and its end intensifies the continuities of nature's rhythms in which we, as mortal creatures, participate. The frame invites us to consider the poem as timeless; the content is nothing if not a meditation on time." The notion of a meditation on time is taken up by Palmer 1981.

27. Ryle 1949, 272–79.

too, from the beginning was in the imaginative mode, and his *nec iam* ("no longer") was not simply a comment on the chronology of the storm and its aftermath but belonged essentially to his way of picturing the landscape. The contrast between then and now was at work from the beginning of the ode. In stanzas 1 to 3, this contrast is the basis of the speaker's encouragement of Thaliarchus. In stanzas 4 to 6, as it is transposed into the times of individual lives, this contrast remains only superficially positive for Thaliarchus, who proves to be the secret sharer in the speaker's age, and it is negative for the somewhat exasperated older man, though neither has cause for regret. Further, Thaliarchus and his companion share the vector of imagination that reaches into the speaker's past and the young man's future and that, the reader feels, pierces beyond the formal beginning and end of the ode. Thaliarchus is summoned not to a single encounter but to many loves (*amores*, 15), to repeated trysts.[28] The pledge might be snatched from either of two parts of one girl's body or from two or more different girls (23–24). As for the speaker, his recollections could go on indefinitely. He could go on, but he stops. Horace thus radically recasts the deontic mode of the senior symposiast as it was received from archaic Greek lyric poetry.

28. *Repetantur*, 20; see *OLD* s.v. 3.

3

. . . .

Third
Reading

The third reading attempts to establish the horizon of expectation of
the ode's original audience and is thus in principle a historical approach of a familiar kind. Much, for example, of Antonio La Penna's
book on Horace and the ideology of the principate takes this approach to the *Odes*.[1] By contrast, the second reading, though it needed
historical support again and again, was not essentially historical, as it
worked within the horizons established by the first, aesthetic reading.
(The first reading itself also needed historical support but remained
perceptual in order to be the basis for the subsequent readings.) The
third reading is, then, a "historicist-reconstructive" one. Jauss's formula for this reading is as follows: it begins "by seeking out the questions (most often unexplicit ones) to which the text was a response
in its time."[2] This response consists of two kinds of expectation, one
based on the literary tradition of the text and the other growing out
of the original readers' questions about the meaning of the text in
relation to their life-world.

As soon as one sets these goals for the historical reading of an
ancient poem, obstacles appear. Ancient response to poetry did not
take the form of interpretations of individual poems, nor, for that

1. La Penna 1963.
2. Jauss 1982, 146.

matter, has modern response done so until about the beginning of the present century. Jauss had to complain of the lack of interpretation contemporary with the publication of Baudelaire's "Spleen II" (1857), though he could rely on Théophile Gautier's foreword to the 1868 edition of *Les fleurs du mal* and on Paul Bourget's chapter on Baudelaire in *Psychologie contemporaine* (1883). The reader of an ancient poem has nothing of the sort and would consider himself blessed if he did. In order to establish the horizon of expectation of C. 1.9's original readers, the reader will have to take a roundabout path, beginning with the place of the ode in the book in which it was published.

The second reading was not intended to correct the first, and the third is not intended to correct the second, as if some true historical understanding could replace the interpretation developed within the aesthetic horizons of the first reading. The principle of Jauss's approach is Hans-Georg Gadamer's critique of historical objectivism. The meaning of the work occurs in the change from the original reader's horizon to that of its present reader, and that is the reason for the historicist-reconstructive reading.[3] Further, other meanings will have been made concrete only in the period intervening between the first reception of the work and the reader's time. Thus the text may, depending on its date of origin and its fortune, have given answers to a whole series of questions, and there arises the possibility of a series of changes between the reader's horizon and that of earlier readers of the text. One surmises that a text as old as C. 1.9 has a long history of reception. Unfortunately, aside from the evidence provided by Porphyrio and pseudo-Acro (to be discussed below), one cannot begin to define particular receptions to this ode, after antiquity, until the Renaissance. In the Middle Ages, Horace's *Satires* and *Epistles* were read far more than his *Odes*, neither

---

3. Jauss 1982, 146: "The reconstruction of the original horizon of expectations would . . . fall back into historicism if the historical interpretation could not in turn serve to transform the question, 'What did the text say?' into the question, 'What does the text say to me, and what do I say to it?' "

the meters nor the contents of which were easily comprehensible.[4] Though allusions, quotations, and occasional imitations show that the Odes never completely disappeared, excerpts in florilegia were the form in which they were known to the readers who knew them at all. In the Renaissance, translations began to appear, and these, studied as readings (as they are in the third section of this chapter), are the first full records of responses to C. 1.9.

Odes 1.9 as the Ninth of the "Parade Odes"

C. 1.1–9 are called the "parade odes" because they introduce the principal meters of the first three books.[5] The ninth is climactic in this sequence. Further, there is general agreement that Horace arranged the odes in books 1–3 according to a plan, though opinions differ on what that plan was. Each ode thus gains significance from its place in the collection. Because the ode under discussion, the ninth in the first book, is in the climactic position in the parade odes, a "dynamic" reading of the ode as it is encountered in sequence is appropriate.[6] This dynamic, progressive reading of C. 1.1–9 is necessarily unlike the aesthetic or interpretive reading of an individual ode, for a sequence, as a process, that is, without closure, could never have the unity of a single ode. At best, the whole collection, culminating in the last ode

4. Manitius 1893; Stemplinger 1913, 2394–96. Quint 1987, 8: "For the Middle Ages, the Roman poet has become the *satiricus*. The existence of his lyric poetry is indeed known, but the interest in it, until the thirteenth century, is very slight."

5. Contrary to a belief recently expressed in print, von Christ (1868) is not the source of the term "parade odes." The origin of the expression may be Teuffel 1920, 55: "B. 1, c. 1–11 bring before the reader all the meters used by Horace in the Odes as in a parade." Teuffel 1920 is the seventh and final edition. The sentence just quoted is not found in the sixth edition.

6. See Santirocco (1986, 24) for the distinction between a static pattern of 1.1–9 and a dynamic, progressive one. Porter (1987, 58–77) discusses C. 1.1–12 as a group organized around the themes of freedom and necessity.

of book 3, might attain some sort of unity, but, on this scale, it would hardly be the unity of a lyric poem.

The sequential reading of the parade odes can expect to notice, besides differences in meter, in addressees, and in subject matter, differences and similarities between the poems in the character or persona of the poet. In the first ode, the naming of the addressee, Maecenas, Horace's patron, would have been enough to identify Horace as the speaker, even without the indications on the outside of and/or at the head of the papyrus roll, and even without the various scenarios of presentation that can be imagined, in which Maecenas and a circle of friends, the primal audience, would have seen and heard that Horace was the source. The speaker of the odes is thus Horace. The distinction between Horace and the speaker observed in the reading of C. 1.9 does not, however, disappear. In C. 1.1 and throughout the *Odes*, when the speaker is to be identified as Horace, it is not always the same Horace. He has different roles to play as speaker of each ode. Horace the speaker will differ from ode to ode in accordance with the addressee and/or the subject. Further, some odes have a speaker who is not necessarily a persona of the poet, not necessarily "Horace." This speaker also differs from ode to ode. Whether it is "Horace" or a nameless speaker, he is always different from the historical Horace. For example, in C. 1.9 the reader encounters Horace the poet as imitator of Alcaeus, but the imitation of Alcaeus is not something that the speaker of that ode is attempting to convey to the addressee, Thaliarchus. Horace and the speaker are both present but clearly distinguishable. This distinction between poet and persona, one of the cornerstones of the New Criticism, remains of great importance for establishing the historical context of the reception of C. 1.9, just as it was for the hermeneutical reading of that ode. For the reading of C. 1.9 in isolation necessarily showed more about the speaker than about Horace, whereas the sequential reading of C. 1.1–9, which can be expected to produce a series of Horaces, will show more about the Horace of C. 1.9. In short, the reader of C. 1.1–9 should expect to discover a series of Horaces none exactly like another.

The distinction between poet and speaker would tend to disappear, however, in a recitation by Horace himself, and, if recitation were the primary historical mode of transmission and hearing were the primary historical reception, it would make little sense to reconstruct an original historical reading. Rather, the reconstruction of the original performance would be the goal of scholarship and interpretation. For, if it could be recovered, the authorial performance would be authoritative on all questions we might ask concerning what for us is a written text. Performance is indeed often considered a norm for Horace's time,[7] and Ovid tells how in his youth he heard Horace reciting the odes:

> et tenuit nostros numerosus Horatius aures,
>   dum ferit Ausonia carmina culta lyra.
>   (Tristia 4.10.49–50)

And Horace, the man of many rhythms, held my ears
enthralled as he struck up songs made on the Ausonian lyre.

And yet Horace distinguishes between two audiences. One is the reader, who holds in his hands his own copy of the odes:

>   iuvat inmemorata ferentem
> ingenuis oculisque legi manibusque teneri.
>   (Epist. 1.19.33–34)

It is my pleasure that I bring things unsung before [he has just spoken of his imitation of Alcaeus] to the nobly born and am read by their eyes and held in their hands.

The other audience is a broader, listening one. Horace proceeds to explain why another kind of reader, the "ungrateful reader" (ingratus . . . lector 35) praises his poems at home and slights them abroad: Horace has never courted public approval; he has never had anything to do with the grammatici, the literary critics of his day;[8] he has avoided

---

7. Quinn 1982, 144–45, 156–57.

8. The lines (39–40) are vexed. My autoschediastic paraphrase falls within the range of acknowledged possibilities.

public recitations (35–47). This passage in *Epistle* 19 makes the claim, then, of writing for the private reader, whose reception of the odes is ocular (*oculis*, 34). Even the detractor is assumed to have the read poems at home. The latter's opposition to Horace is the result, however, of the poet's refusal to observe the conventions of contemporary literary life, which apparently required recitation as a show of deference to some broader public opinion and also concessions of some sort to the importance of the *grammatici*.[9]

   Epistle 13 provides a clear example of a primary reception of the odes by a reader. Horace consigns his odes to a certain Vinius for delivery to Augustus. He cautions the man against disgracing himself, and thus the gift, before Augustus. These are poems *quae possint oculos auresque morari / Caesaris* (17–18), "that may give pause to the eyes and ears of Caesar." Again, the primary reception is ocular, though *aures* assumes that Augustus either will read the poems aloud or will subvocalize his reading and hear the poems with his inner ear. The historicity of *Epistle* 13 does not affect the present argument. Even if Vinius and his mission are completely fictitious, Horace has shown how he imagined a possible reception of his odes. In short, his odes would be read.

   One can add the point that the careful arrangement of the odes in books 1–3 presupposes reading and rereading.[10] Even if whole books of the *Odes* were recited on a single occasion, no listening audience could grasp even the more modest of the patterns that have been discovered. And even in the case of the recitation or performance of a single ode by Horace or someone else, the interpretation of the speaker's voice and attitude would differ from one reciter to another and from one occasion to another. The reciter of C. 1.8, for example, might "play" the speaker's attitude as annoyed and exasperated (you have done it again; stop seducing young Roman noblemen) or mildly reproving (I know you can't help it, but you should try to stop). Horace himself might have recited the same ode differ-

9. On whom see Quinn 1982, 151; Kenney 1982, 33–37.
10. Cf. Quinn 1982, 143–44.

ently on different occasions. The still vexed question of the punctuation of the first sentence of C. 1.9 may go back to an original ambivalence. Horace himself might have inflected the sentence now as a question, now as a declarative statement. Such varying historical performances of the *Odes* would presuppose an interpretation, or at least a decision, prior to the performance, and they therefore show that a reading of some sort is in every case primary. An original unity of Horace and the speaker of an ode is only a mirage. The original condition of reception was, as it is for us, interpretation, in which Horace himself would have participated whenever he read or discussed his odes. In each ode, there was an irreducible element of Horace, distinguishable from the speaker—that originality, for example, in the history of Roman literature to which he himself liked to call attention (C. 3.30.12–14; Epist. 19.21–34) or one of his repeated, programmatic themes. There was also an ingredient of the speaker, always changing, because different readers, whether silent ones or readers-aloud or translators, have always made and will always make different choices among the various responses that each ode may elicit.

In the sequential approach to be taken here, a double reading of each ode becomes possible: a hermeneutical reading, like the one demonstrated in the two preceding chapters, which is more responsive to the speaker, and a contextual reading, which is more responsive to the poet and the personas of the poet. For example, the speaker's advice to Thaliarchus in C. 1.9 concerning love contrasts with the attitude toward love of the speaker in the preceding ode, and this contrast belongs to a larger polarization of views on the relationship between the public and the private that is established in the first two odes and elaborated in the odes intervening between the second and the ninth. In this development, the reader becomes aware of the poet's (as distinguished from any particular speaker's) preoccupations. The contextual reading of C. 1.9 thus brings out concerns that the original audience might have felt or noticed but that are invisible to the reader of the ode in isolation. The double reading thus helps to define both that which is idiosyncratic and/or unhistorical in the hermeneutical response and also that which bridges the horizons of the hermeneutical interpreter and the ode's first audience.

The first ode expresses Horace's gratitude to his patron, Maecenas, and declares his identity and his aspirations as a lyric poet. The second laments the wickedness of the present generation and declares the poet's allegiance to the heaven-sent savior, Octavian. The first word of the first ode is Maecenas; the last word of the second ode is Caesar (that is, Octavian). The first two odes thus establish an opposition between the poet's personal concerns, expressed in C. 1.1 (*meum*, 2; *me*, 29; *me*, 30; *me*, 35), and his civic concerns in C. 1.2 (*vidimus*, 13; *precamur*, 30; *nostris*, 47; the first person singular does not occur). This polarity is already present in C. 1.1, in which the foils to the poet's life include the life of the Roman statesman (7–8). And it is as poet that Horace presents himself. He is not merely offering a book of poems (cf. Catullus 1; Tibullus 1.1, 2.1); he is speaking as a poet whose hope to be included among the great lyric poets is still to be confirmed (note the future tenses in 30 and 36). What he will be is a *lyricus vates*. The combination of Greek adjective and Roman noun (indicating a specifically Roman concept of the poet) in this phrase is programmatic,[11] though at this point the phrase *lyricus vates* seems straightforward enough: Horace would like to be classed with the canonical nine lyric poets of Greece. The Roman element thus seems to be subordinated to the Greek. On the other hand, Horace's use of the priamel,[12] which has unmistakable Greek antecedents, brings in various distinctly Roman ways of life.[13] The relation of the Greek and Roman elements is already complex.

The third ode, a propempticon, returns to a personal concern, the safety of the poet's friend, Vergil, who has undertaken a trip to Athens. The ode begins as a prayer to the ship that bears him (1–8).

---

11. Bundy 1986, 5: "The priamel is a focusing or selecting device in which one or more terms serve as foil for the point of particular interest."

12. McDermott 1977 and 1981.

13. Nisbet and Hubbard 1970, 2–3.

The poet then reflects on the bravery of the first man who put a ship to sea (9–20), a bravery that then turns out to be impiety, because divine forethought separated the lands by means of the ocean, which ships ought not to touch (21–24). This observation leads the poet to a more general reflection on the propensity of the human race to challenge all limits, and he gives as examples Prometheus' theft of fire, Daedalus' flight, and Hercules' incursion into the underworld (25–40). Vergil's presumably innocent and unassuming trip to Athens thus comes to be associated with the most famous acts of defiance of human limitations. The moral concerns of the second ode have been deflated as the poet turns to high joking.[14] In the first stanza of C. 1.2, Juppiter's thunder was a portent showing his displeasure at the civil strife of the Romans; in the last stanza of C. 1.3, Juppiter's thunder is the climax of the humorous expansion of the propempticon to the poet's friend. The propempticon has been soon abandoned (after the first eight of forty lines), and, as in C. 1.1, the Greek model or models hardly confine the poet, who, as poet (as distinguished from speaker), seems to be commenting on their banality.

In C. 1.4, for the first time in the sequence, Horace takes the stance of adviser and tells Lucius Sestius, consul suffectus in the year in which *Odes* 1–3 were published, to enjoy life while he may (13–14). Though he is rich, he is equal to a poor man before inevitable death. Horace's advice is introduced against the background of the coming of spring (1–8). The new season invites to feasting: put on garlands of green myrtle or of the flowers the earth now releases; sacrifice to Faunus in shady groves (9–12). The countryside outside Rome is the imagined setting, and the scene entails the implicit exhortation to leave the city and its cares. At the end of the ode, the invitation to feasting is restated in more specific terms: after you have entered the house of Pluto, you will no longer participate in symposia nor will you gaze upon the tender Lycidas (16–20). (Lycidas, the first Greek

14. Seidensticker (1976, 30), however, reads C. 1.3 as completely serious, as he wants to connect it with C. 1.1 and to set C. 1.4–9 apart as a group arranged in a certain order.

name in the *Odes*, could stand either for any attractive young man or for Sestius' attachment of the moment.) Wine and love and, implicitly, forgetfulness of cares are thus the substance of the admonition to Sestius. Love makes an explicit entrance into the odes for the first time. It was present from the first, however, in the poet's association of himself with the dances of nymphs and satyrs:[15]

> me gelidum nemus
>
> Nympharumque leves cum Saturis chori
> secernunt populo
>
> (C. 1.1.30–32)

The cool grove and the light-hearted dances of the nymphs and satyrs set me apart from the mob.

The adjective *leves* ("light-hearted") will be Horace's own sobriquet (*C.* 1.6.20). And in the second ode, in the list of divinities whom the Roman people might call upon for aid, there appears *Erycina ridens, / quam Iocus circum volat et Cupido* (*C.* 1.2.33–34) ("laughing (Venus) Erycina about whom Jest and Cupid flit")—a curious amatory image in the context of serious political concerns, one sanctioned by the fact that Venus is the mother of Aeneas, the ancestor of the Romans, and should thus be interested in their fate.

The general program of emulation of Greek lyric poetry, expressed in *C.* 1.1.32–36, might have led the reader to expect the themes of love and the symposium that appear in *C.* 1.4. The second and third odes showed that Horace had to present other faces first. In *C.* 1.2 he established his good faith as a citizen (the lines on Venus just quoted are only two of fifty-two); the moralizing of that ode was continued in *C.* 1.3 but in a jocular tone. Only in *C.* 1.4 do themes that will prove characteristic emerge explicitly, and for the first time the opposition between public and private is framed, albeit indirectly,

---

15. I owe this observation and some others to Pöschl (1986). My own conclusions concerning love in *C.* 1.1–9 differ considerably from his, however, as will be seen.

within a single ode. That curious solitary figure in C. 1.1, the man who did not shun to steal part of the day for cups of Massic wine, lying beneath arbutus or by the side of a spring (19–22), now begins to come into his own. Except that, unlike Sestius, he had no Lycidas nearby.[16]

C. 1.4 ends with the tender (*tenerum*, 19) boy Lycidas; C. 1.5 begins with a slip of a boy (*gracilis puer*, 1). This boy presses Pyrrha on a bed of roses—like Lycidas, she has a Greek name and, like him, is beloved. With its theme of love, C. 1.5 is especially apt for a double reading. The speaker of this ode offers himself as an example of shipwrecked passion, and this example provides a (stylistically brilliant) conclusion to the ode. In the context of the parade odes, however, the speaker of C. 1.5 is one of the personae of Horace: the lyric poet as lover or ex-lover (and, as usual, dexterous, liberated imitator of Greek antecedents). This self-representation by the poet fits with one of the two spheres of activity designated by the poet of the preceding ode (C. 1.4) as the pleasures of this life, namely, love, the other being the convivium (18–20). The convivium entails friendship, already expressed by the poet of C. 1.3 toward Vergil (*animae dimidium meae*). The sequence of C. 1.3–5—friendship, symposium, love—thus provides a rough answer to a question posed by the enumeration of ways of life in C. 1.1: what is the way of life of the *lyricus vates*? Or, what is entailed in his choice of life as compared with mine?

C. 1.6, then, explicitly contrasting Horace's poetry with epic, specifies convivia and love as its two themes (17–19) and lack of seriousness (*leves*, 20) as its ethos. In this poem, Horace addresses Marcus Vipsanius Agrippa, the most powerful man in Rome after Octavian, with whom he is associated in line 11, refusing to write an epic on his exploits, a task better left to the epic poet Lucius Varius Rufus. Horace speaks as one close to Octavian's court—he has already addressed L. Sestius on familiar terms—and as a poet who might have a public role to play. He remains detached, however (*vacui*, 19).

16. See Nisbet and Hubbard 1970, 61, for the fusion of Greek and Roman elements in C. 1.4.

Nevertheless, in refusing to pay Agrippa and Augustus the honor they would receive from epic, he pays it to them in lyric when he associates them with the heroes of Homeric epic as belonging to a class of subjects far beyond him. And in his detachment he is close enough to the center of the new regime to address his lyric poems to its most powerful men. In this way, Horace's detachment and levity themselves become political; the *recusatio* is as much a political as a poetic gesture. The emergence of a Roman lyric poetry out of Greek lyric (and other) poetry is, at the same time, the establishment of a distance from Roman public concerns. Horace's own passions (note *sive quid urimur*, 19), part of the program of his lyric poetry, are not simply private; they are asserted against other claims on his attention and time. Again the fainéant of C. 1.1 comes to mind, whose way of life was unlike any of the others in its complete inactivity (except for drinking and the implication of movement from arbutus to springside) and detachment. His chosen locale and detachment had something in common with the poet's (with C. 1.6.19–22 cf. C. 1.30–32, especially *gelidum nemus* and *secernunt populo*). Again, however, as in C. 1.4, in contrast with the fainéant's complete tranquillity, the reader notices erotic passion as an intrusive element (note *urimur*, with which *vacui* in the same line is in implicit contrast, as I argue below).

C. 1.7 takes up one of the two lyric themes specified in the preceding ode, convivia, but in a paraenetic mode, addressing Lucius Munatius Plancus, another member of Octavian's inner circle. The poem begins with a priamel, the focus of which is the poet's choice of Tibur (Tivoli) as a subject of song more appealing than any of the great cities of Greece (1–14). By an oblique Pindaric movement, he turns to Plancus, who should remember to use wine to end his troubles, whether on military duty or in his (native, according to Porphyrio) Tibur (15–21)—Tibur turns out to be the connection between the first two parts of the poem. Then the poet gives a mythical exemplum: Teucer, when he was banished from Salamis by his father, exhorted his colleagues to drive away their cares with wine (22–32). Like many Pindaric exempla, this one makes its point by emphasizing an unexpected detail in the myth, here the convivium that took place on the night before Teucer and his companions had to leave Salamis for parts unknown. The Pindaric quality of the ode is not maintained to the end, however, as the poet never reverts to Plancus; and, for that matter, he has never singled out any exploit or even any quality of Plancus to praise. Nevertheless, even the incomplete imitation of the Pindaric victory ode tacitly confers honor on Plancus, at the same time that Horace reestablishes the persona of C. 1.4, in which he reminded Sestius of the main pleasures of this life. In other words, the Pindaric imitation has two functions—to praise Plancus and, through its deliberate imperfection, to open the way to a characteristically Horatian paraenesis. The Roman Horace emerges against the background of the Greek model and, in so doing, still maintains a certain relationship with a powerful man; a persona, which harks back to the Massic-quaffing fainéant of C. 1.1, reasserts itself.

C. 1.8 turns to the other of the two themes specified in 1.6, love. The poet addresses a certain Lydia, either one of those *virgines acres* (C. 1.6.17–18) or another Pyrrha (C. 1.5). He asks her a series of mock-surprised questions. What have you done to Sybaris that he now shuns the Campus and avoids military training, swimming, and sports? The climactic question compares him to Achilles on Scyros disguised by his mother in women's clothing so that he would not have to go to Troy.[17] Sybaris is in hiding (*latet*, 13); he is not seen in public places, among his peers, engaged in the activities in which he was once conspicuous (*nobilis*, 12). This ode thus gives a particular sense to the antithesis between the public and the private and even enumerates various public Roman activities that love repudiates. The speaker of this ode is indignant and thus implicitly—it is hard to tell how seriously—aligns himself with traditional Roman values. He could be the same man who suffered the shipwreck of his passion for Pyrrha and has learned his lesson. He is certainly represented as close to Lydia, close enough to play the role of Dutch uncle. What is

---

17. Santirocco 1986, 41: C. 1.6 gives a "program for lyric as opposed to epic," and C. 1.7–8 "enact that program by domesticating epic material in the service of convivia and erotica respectively."

the attitude of Horace, as distinguished from the speaker and situation Horace represents to the reader? The Horace who took the *proelia virginum* (again, C. 1.6.17–18) as his subject did so in opposition to the lofty themes of epic and to the obligation to praise the deeds of the Roman general Marcus Agrippa; and he counseled L. Sestius, consul suffectus, to enjoy the sight of Lycidas while he could. Now, in C. 1.8, he seems to take another view of the matter. Whereas the speaker's attitude toward love can be established in each ode, Horace's is less certain because his persona changes from ode to ode.

In the historical context for the reading of C. 1.9 that emerges from the sequential reading of C. 1.1–8, love is the more emphasized and the more problematical of the two spheres, love and symposium, to which lyric poetry is devoted. Love thus complicates the basic question of way of life which was posed by C. 1.1 and to which the sequence C. 1.2–8 offered various answers. To the question, What life should I choose? to which these poems responded, is added the second question, How should I live the life that I have chosen? or, more precisely, What should be the role of love in the life that I lead? In this historical context, certain aspects of C. 1.9 take on far greater prominence than they had in the first two readings. The two activities proposed for Thaliarchus, *amores* and dancing, and the two venues, the Campus and *areae*, now can be seen as alternatives. The Campus, which would be the site of Thaliarchus' dancing, was the scene of Sybaris' healthy endeavors, before he fell in love (C. 1.8.4). The speaker of C. 1.9, having mentioned the Campus and then *areae*, is carried away by thoughts of love. In the historical context, the reader would have responded, not primarily to the problem of time and age, as the hermeneutical reading offered above in chapters 1 and 2 has done, but to the assertion of love as a worthy pursuit for the young man to whom the ode is addressed. The ancient reader would have been more aware of the persona of Horace, who in a similar persona had announced as one of his themes just those *proelia virginum* (again, C. 1.6.17–18), of which the last stanza of C. 1.9 is an example. The ancient reader would also, in this regard, have been more responsive to the implied preference of love over convivium, as the speaker directs the thoughts of Thaliarchus away from the setting and their friendship to springtime trysts.

Horace's relation in C. 1.9 to the literary tradition in which he is working reinforces the emphasis on love that emerges in the historical reading. To put the matter somewhat crudely, not only is this emphasis un-Roman, it is also un-Greek or at least un-Alcaic. A recommendation to a young man to seek relationships with girls is unimaginable in Alcaeus' poems.[18] Their orientation to the poet's life and circumstances is completely different from that of Horace to his. Alcaeus is politically engaged: without the hetaireia, the male club, there is no Alcaic lyric.[19] In the milieu of this poetry, one of the most characteristic forms of group solidarity was the symposium, the poetic representation of which included expressions of pederastic feeling.[20] The fragments of Alcaeus show only the phrases "sitting beside Deinomenes" (frag. 376 Lobel-Page) and "dear boy" (ὦ φίλε παῖ, frag. 366 Lobel-Page) and two indubitably pederastic lines preserved without the name of their author, which Bergk attributed to Alcaeus (frag. 368 Lobel-Page). But Cicero's remark concerning Alcaeus, *quae de iuvenum amore scripsit* (*Tusc.* 4.71; cf. *N.D.* 1.79), and Horace's reference to Lycus as Alcaeus' beloved (C. 1.32.11–12) are enough to complete the picture. The Alcaean symposium would have been, in this respect, much like the Theognidean one, in which politics and pederasty are intertwined.[21]

In order to show the relation of C. 1.9 to the pederasty that can be assumed for its Alcaic model, I begin by returning to C. 1.4, in which the reminder to Sestius of life's brevity is associated with his love of the boy Lycidas:

18. See Rösler 1980, 235–38, on Alcaeus' attitude toward women.

19. To paraphrase Rösler 1980, 40.

20. Pederasty is denied by Page (1955, 294–95); doubted by Rösler (1980, 244 n. 321); asserted by Gentili (in Gentili and Perrotta 1965, 219). Pasquali (1920, 83) said of Alcaeus, in comparison with C. 1.9, "The bold knight will rather have loved a young squire than a courtesan and with a simple, rough love that will not have delighted in joking of the kind we find here [in C. 1.9]."

21. Edmunds 1988, 83–84.

Iam te premet nox fabulaeque manes

et domus exilis Plutonia, quo simul mearis,
   nec regna vini sortiere talis,
nec tenerum Lycidan mirabere, quo calet iuventus
   nunc omnis et mox virgines tepebunt.

(C. 1.4.16–20)

Soon night will close around you and the fabled shades,
and the poor house of Pluto, whither once you go,
you'll neither cast the dice to choose the drinking's arbiter,
nor feast your eyes on tender Lycidas, for whom men all are
      ardent now
And girls will soon begin to warm.

These are the final lines of the ode, which thus ends with a précis of Lycidas' erotic biography. He is now an *eromenos*, the object of pederastic attention, but soon girls will be interested in him (and he will be interested in them and no longer in you, Sestius). Horace finds the most poignant way to express to Sestius the passage of time. Against the Alcaic background, for which a pederastic relationship between speaker and addressee can be assumed, the situation in C. 1.9 appears to be exactly the same as in C. 1.4,[22] except that there is a complete ellipse of the thought that Thaliarchus is no longer an *eromenos* (a thought supplied by the medieval scholiast who called Thaliarchus *puer speciosus*), as the speaker must make the argument that Thaliarchus is still young. While Thaliarchus hears this message, the reader, in virtue of the Alcaic model, hears from Horace another message: Thaliarchus is getting older; one erotic stage of his life has al-

---

22. So far as I know, the only scholar to have made this observation is Williams (1980, 202): "who is Thaliarchus? He is addressed with the emotional o, and this should not just be dismissed as a Grecism that goes with his Greek name. It sounds as if Thaliarchus might be a beloved of the poet's who has reached that time in life when, by a convention recognised at least in ancient literature, a youth shifts his interest from men to girls." Williams cites C. 1.4 but does not relate his observation to Alcaeus.

ready passed. This dimension of the poem would have been grasped much more easily by Horace's contemporary readers than it is by us, who have so little of the pederastic poetry of Alcaeus. They knew what Cicero was talking about.

Both Bernd Seidensticker and Viktor Pöschl have observed the contrasting attitudes toward love in C. 1.4 and 5 and in C. 1.8 and 9, and their articles provide sufficient evidence for an almost systematic deployment of the theme of love in the parade odes.[23] But Horace did not present this theme as a "whole full of tension."[24] First, the theme is not a whole. Neither marriage nor the relation of love and marriage is considered. A Roman would not necessarily have connected the two, but even Lucretius allowed the possibility of conjugal love (consuetudo concinnat amorem, 4.1283) and Juvenal curiously regarded love as the expected, though unattainable (because of women's impudicitia), condition of marriage:

> Si tibi legitimis pactam iunctamque libellis
> non es amaturus, ducendi nulla videtur
> causa
>
> (6.200–202)

If you are not going to love the one betrothed and joined to you in law, there is no good reason to marry.

In the parade odes, Horace does not consider this form of love. Second, Horace presents contrasts not only in attitude, positive or negative, toward love (the analyses of Seidensticker and Pöschl remain at this abstract level) but also in kinds of love. Horace, in effect, encourages Sestius to enjoy Lycidas while he can; the speaker of C. 1.9 encourages the youth Thaliarchus to pursue girls. Further, the parade odes implicitly distinguish between female love objects: freedwomen or courtesans like Pyrrha and freeborn Roman girls like those Thaliarchus will meet in the areae of Rome.[25]

---

23. Seidensticker 1976; Pöschl 1986.

24. "Spannungsreiches Ganzes": Pöschl 1986, 68.

25. The puella of C. 1.9 cannot be a meretrix. See Pasquali 1920, 84.

Is it possible to arrive at any conclusion concerning Horace's own views on love? In C. 1.6, the speaker, a persona of Horace, specifies *quid urimur* (19) as one of his themes. But *quid* tells nothing about the object of the passion and perhaps leaves various possibilities open—male, freeborn or slave, and female, freeborn or slave or freedwoman or courtesan. Various apparently autobiographical passages in Horace's oeuvre suggest some answers.[26] But here I am attempting to put C. 1.9 in the context of the theme of love as it emerges in the parade odes in order to get a sense of Horace's contemporaries' response to the advice given Thaliarchus. To return to C. 1.6.17–20, the verb *urimur* by itself might make one think of Catullus (72.5), Tibullus (2.4.6), Sulpicia (5.5), or Ovid (*Am.* 1.1.26)—of an obsessive passion beside which all other commitments become unimportant, a passion, moreover, with which the role of poet or poetess is integral. In listing *convivia, proelia virginum,* and *quid urimur* as his themes, Horace might seem to associate himself with the ethos of the Roman elegiac poets. And yet he says, *cantamus vacui,* whereas in the works of these poets love invades the person who is *vacuus* and puts an end to the carefree state: *uror, et in vacuo pectore regnat Amor* (Ovid, *loc. cit.*). One who can say of himself *uror* is no longer *vacuus*. Horace's line, *cantamus vacui, sive quid urimur* . . . (C. 1.6.19), judged from the perspective of the love poets, contains a contradiction. One cannot both burn with love and be free.[27] *Uror* could, however, refer to brief infatuations (Ovid *Am.* 2.4.12), and perhaps these are what should be assumed for the Horatian persona of the parade odes, though the speaker of C. 1.5 has suffered the shipwreck of a grand passion for Pyrrha. Horace as poet of love in the parade odes has different advice for different addressees. His very lack of commitment, of seriousness, seems to be the message. The variety itself of erotic possibilities might prevent commitment. Though it is sometimes said that moral seriousness was expected of the group around Maecenas,[28] it is lacking in the parade

26. See Shackleton Bailey 1982, 41–42.
27. In C. 1.5.10 *vacuam* means "free of other commitments."
28. Quinn 1982, 141.

odes (except for C. 1.8, which is not terribly grave), and, to judge by
Seneca's description of Maecenas (*Ep.* 114.4–6), Maecenas would not
have been offended.

Intertextuality

In this third, historical reading of C. 1.9, as in the first two readings,
the Alcaic model (338 Lobel-Page), and in particular Horace's devia-
tion from the assumed pederasty of that model, has again become
significant as putatively belonging to the experience of the original
audience. This aspect of the Alcaic model did not enter into the first
two readings because of its remoteness from the present reader, who
recovered it only after a series of reflections that were, in fact, initiated
by Jauss's stipulations for the third reading. The subject of pederasty
in C. 1.9 has, for that matter, been seldom discussed. This particular
aspect of the literary tradition of C. 1.9 came into the discussion apropos of the theme of love in C. 1.1–9, a theme that would have responded to a question concerning its life-world in the mind of the
original audience. But the literary tradition of C. 1.9 is operative in this
poem in many other ways, and its elaborate intertextuality with other
poems and even with works of art remains to be considered.

If, however, C. 1.9 has such a degree of intertextuality, the question immediately arises why it did not enter into the second reading
or even the first, in which a certain amount of historical information
was already assumed. As for the first reading, it was to some extent
guided by the poem's similarities to and differences from the Alcaic
model, which might be called its direct tradition, but, following Jauss,
the first reading attempted to hear the poem in the versification and
to discern a unity in the relationship of the speaker to the addressee.
A reading along these lines proved to be possible. The interpretive
questions left over for the second reading did not, as it happened,
lead into the poem's intertextual dimension. Many of these questions
were explored and answered without philology and literary history.
Now, in the third reading, which is addressed to the original audi-

ence's expectations, what might be called the poem's indirect tradition—to which the original audience would have been more sensitive than twentieth-century readers—will be pursued.

The fundamental tendency of Horace's use of the direct tradition has already become clear: he invokes a certain model only to
reshape it and finally to abandon it. Further, this tendency, as the
main development of C. 1.9 clearly shows, is specifically toward what
might be called the Romanization of Horace's poem in keeping, first
of all, with his explicit *aemulatio*. Already in the second stanza, this
tendency emerges. It was observed in the first reading that, in comparison with Alcaeus, Horace gives a fuller prescription for the serving
of the wine. The intertextuality of this passage with Greek antecedents
is even overdetermined, in that the wine is not only the wine of the
Alcaic model but also is four years old, a bucolic, Theocritean wine
(cf. *Id.* 7.147; 14.15–16) suited to the country setting. The jar has a
Greek name, *diota*. And yet the jar itself is local (*Sabina*), and so is the
wine itself. In the course of a fairly close imitation of Alcaeus (as
emerged from the first reading), Horace says, in effect, drink native,
that is, be native, be Roman. This message is one that comes from the
code operative between Horace and the reader and issues from Horace's *aemulatio*, his desire to become the Roman Alcaeus.[29]

This *aemulatio* operates, further, in broader intertextual dimensions, in less direct traditions. One of these is Lucretius and Epicureanism; another is the symposium theme in Roman literature and
art. In both of these, Horace will be found to be defining, in and for
his own poem, a position alternative to the ones his allusions evoke.
In this way, the poetic *aemulatio* finally encompasses the definition of
a new ethics, and one of the original audience's sets of expectations,
based on the literary tradition of the text, is addressed at the same
time as the other, based on the meaning of the text in relation to that
audience's life-world.

29. For an explicit statement of rivalry with Alcaeus see the index in Borzsák
1984, s.v. Alcaeus. For discussion of these and related passages cf. Reiff 1959,
51–73.

An Epicureanism emerges in the advice of the speaker to Thaliarchus in the second stanza, in particular in the Lucretian cast of some elements of the diction. *Dissolvo, -ere* is a favorite Lucretian verb (forty-odd examples), and *cetera* (again, forty-odd examples, in the nominative or accusative) is a favorite Lucretian summary term. *Fuge quaerere* reminds one of Lucretius' *fuge credere, Memmi* (1.1052), the unique occurrence of *fuge* in Lucretius, in a line that has something of the same intensity of line 13 in C. 1.9. Horace's storm (stanza 3) seems to be indebted to Lucretian storms. The main components of Horace's storm (*ventos, aequore fervido*) appear, for example, in Lucretius' comparison of an epileptic fit to a storm:

> turbat agens anima spumas, ⟨ut⟩ in <u>aequore</u> salso
> <u>ventorum</u> validis <u>fer</u>vescunt viribus undae.
>
> (3.493–94)

His (that of the man seized by the fit) soul is in turmoil and breaks into foam (at the mouth), as on the salt sea the waves seethe through the stout strength of the winds.

With Horace's personification of the winds (*deproeliantis*, 11) compare Lucretius' *validis . . . viribus.* Further, the thought of line 13 has a clear parallel in the Epicurean philosopher Philodemus (*De morte* IV, col. 38).[30] In sum, the reader is given the sense that, along with the transposition of the Alcaic setting from Lesbos or Thrace to the countryside outside Rome, the relationship between speaker and addressee has been recast in a Roman Epicurean mold.

At the same time, the reader is aware of distinctly non-Epicurean notions. Horace's gods calm the winds. In Lucretius' exposition of the philosophy of Epicurus, the winds and all such phenomena are to be understood naturalistically (6.96–534). While Lucretius concentrates on thunder and lightning, he mentions snow, wind, hail, frost, and ice as obeying the same natural laws he has set forth (6.527–

---

30. Lebek 1981, 2042–43. (Paratore 1973, 201–2, has only general reflections on Horace and Epicureanism.)

34). The peaceful gods of Lucretius, dwelling apart in the *intermundia*, could not be expected to have anything to do with the weather. Horace's *permitte divis cetera* is popular and traditional. But the speaker of C. 1.9 is farthest from Lucretius in the advice of the fourth and fifth stanzas. "Do not spurn love" is diametrically opposed to Lucretius' *decet . . . pabula amoris / absterrere sibi et alio convertere* mentem ("you should drive away from you what feeds your love and turn your mind somewhere else," 4.1064–65), a precept that occurs near the beginning of his lengthy attack on sexual love (4.1058–1287).[31]

The reader does not mishear Epicurean-Lucretian overtones in C. 1.9. Rather, as in other aspects of the ode, a sorting out and correction of impressions take place, as the speaker's intent becomes clearer or as Horace distances himself from the intellectual tradition he has evoked. The pursuit of love, it turns out, is the climax of the speaker's advice to Thaliarchus, and love is in contradiction to the at least potentially Epicurean, self-sufficient security of the fireside and to the potentially Epicurean friendship of the speaker and Thaliarchus, itself a revision of the *philia* that can be assumed for the Alcaic model.

Another dimension of the intertextuality of C. 1.9 is a particular sympotic theme in Roman art and poetry. In the course of his demonstration of the folly of the fear of death, Lucretius takes an example of the expression of this fear in everyday life, in particular, at the convivium:

hoc etiam faciunt ubi discubuere tenentque
pocula saepe homines et inumbrant ora coronis,
ex animo ut dicant "brevis hic est fructus homullis;
iam fuerit neque post umquam revocare licebit."
(Lucr. 3.912–15)

This, too, men often do when they recline and hold
their cups and shade their brows with garlands:

---

31. For Epicurus' "On Love," with quotation of fragments, see Bailey 1966, 1303.

from the heart they say, "Brief is this pleasure for us mannikins; soon it will be gone and never can we call it back again."

The point of Lucretius' example is the intrusion of the fear of death into the midst of joy. That the thought of death was conventional at the banquet or convivium and took a particular, conventional form appears from a passage in the Cena Trimalchionis "Banquet of Trimalchio" in the Satyricon of Petronius. During the banquet, the host has a jointed, silver skeleton brought in. He forms it into various postures on the table in front of him and then delivers these verses:

eheu nos miseros, quam totus homuncio nil est!
sic erimus cuncti, postquam nos auferet Orcus.
ergo vivamus, dum licet esse bene.

> (Petr. 34.10)

Alas, what wretches we are! Take him for all in all, a mere man
is nothing!
We'll all be thus after Orcus carries us off.
Therefore let's live, as long as it's ours to enjoy life.

We'll all be like this skeleton, Trimalchio says. The survival of several of these model skeletons (though not in silver) shows that the scene in the Satyricon had a basis in real life.[32] The sentiment expressed by Trimalchio is the same conventional one to which Lucretius refers.

The origin of the skeleton at the banquet may have been Egyptian (cf. Hdt. 2.78; Plut. Mor. 357F). In a group of late Hellenistic ceramics, the skeleton makes its appearance as a reveler. One of these, from southern Thrace, which also has the paraphernalia for a banquet, bears the inscription κτῶ χρῶ ("get what you can, enjoy it while you may").[33] This slogan is found on gems and grave inscriptions as well. By the time of Horace C. 1.9, the theme had appeared in Roman

---

32. For a survey of the evidence for the skeletons see Dunbabin 1986.
33. Dunbabin 1986, 99. The translation is hers.

art.[34] The most notable examples are two silver cups in the Boscoreale treasure, which have both skulls and skeletons. While the iconography is extremely complicated, the inscriptions make at least one message clear. One cup has ζῶν μετάλαβε τὸ γὰρ αὔριον ἄδηλόν ἐστι ("take your share while you're alive; for tomorrow is uncertain") and τέρπε ζῶν σεα[υ]τόν ("enjoy yourself while you're alive"). The other has εὐφραίνου ὃν ζῆς χρόνον ("be merry for the time that you live").

Death is the threat and the stimulus to the joys of the convivium. In the pseudo-Vergilian *Copa*, the hostess of a tavern invites a wayfarer to come into her garden out of the summer heat. She promises delightful food and drink. Put on garlands. There is a girl for you to kiss. The hostess concludes:

> quid cineri ingrato servas bene olentia serta?
>   anne coronato vis lapide ista tegi?
> pone merum et talos. pereat qui crastina curat.
>   mors aurem vellens "vivite" ait "venio."
>
>   (*Copa* 35–38)

Why save the fragrant garlands for your thankless ashes?
Or do you wish them to be covered over and your tombstone
    crowned instead of you?
Set wine and dice before you. Perish the one who cares about
    tomorrow.
Death plucks your ear and says, "Live, I am coming."

The thought of the uncertain tomorrow (*crastina*; cf. *C.* 1.9.13, *cras*) is the thought of death.[35] *Ambulat et subito funus mirantur amici*—"he's walking around, and, all of a sudden, his friends are marveling at his fu-

---

34. Dunbabin 1986, 232–33: "The weight of the present evidence would . . . suggest that the skull allegory was in use, and associated with the symposium, by the middle decades of the first century B.C. at the very latest; and that both the inanimate and the animated skeleton themes developed at approximately the same time or very shortly thereafter, and were in common use by early in the reign of Augustus."

35. The theme persists in Martial 2.59 and 5.64.

neral" (Prop. 2.4.13). The leaves that fall from our garlands into our wine cups are reminders that the next day may be our last:

ac veluti folia arentes liquere corollas,
    quae passim calathis strata natare vides,
sic nobis, qui nunc magnum speramus amantes,
    forsitan includet crastina fata dies.
                        (Prop. 2.15.51–54)

And like the leaves fallen from withered garlands
that you see strewn about and floating in our cups,
so for us lovers, who now have great hopes,
perhaps tomorrow will close our doom.

The theme of death and the convivium entails the renunciation of all thought of tomorrow, even the most urgent thought, that of the lover. Note again *crastina . . . dies*.

    In this survey of other sympotic texts, both a basic similarity to and a basic difference from C. 1.9 have emerged. The similarity lies in the uncertainty of tomorrow. With "What will happen—tomorrow—shun to ask" (C. 1.9.13), compare the Greek vase inscriptions quoted above and the references to tomorrow in some of the Latin passages. The difference lies in the thought of death that is expressed in various ways in these other texts, most notably in the skeleton at the convivium. For the opposition life-death, C. 1.9 substitutes the opposition youth-age. This poem suppresses a thought that was conventional not only in the artistic and poetic representations of the convivium but also apparently in the real-life convivium and thus would have been present in the mind of the ancient reader.

The Ancient and Modern Titles of *Odes* 1.9

An index of a certain modern response—but not the one demonstrated in the first two readings above—is the title that C. 1.9 has acquired: "The Soracte Ode."[36] With this modern title, one can contrast the title, or titles, that began to appear in late antiquity and that are found in many medieval manuscripts of Horace. These titles, at least some of them indices of relatively ancient response, appear in the commentaries of Porphyrio, of perhaps the fourth century,[37] and pseudo-Acro. The copyists sometimes record their source for a title—Horace himself (that is, a manuscript of Horace known to the copyist), Acro, Porphyrio, or two of the three. Exactly when these titles came into use is impossible to say; but they belong to a stage in the reception of the *Odes* that is historically distinguishable from Horace's own time. For, despite the belief of the copyists, if Horace or one of his contemporaries wanted to refer to a particular ode, he used the first line as a "title" (cf. Verg. Ec. 5.85–87).[38]

The comparison of the modern and the ancient titles brings together the first (at all) definable response after Horace's time and a modern response (to the extent that it can be inferred from the title "The Soracte Ode" alone) just antecedent to the one I myself have given in chapters 1 and 2. My response differs considerably, in ways that will become clear, from the response epitomized in the title "The Soracte Ode." The ancient and modern titles thus represent two stages of response falling in between that of Horace's contemporaries (the first section of this chapter) and that of the late twentieth-century Jaussian reader (the first two chapters of this book). The translations to be studied in the final section of this chapter represent yet another stage, beginning before and then overlapping the stage epitomized

36. The ode is thus referred to in the title of scholarly articles: Baneke 1963–64; Connor 1972; Esler 1968–69; Gelsomino 1962; Haffter 1972; Moritz 1976; Moskovit 1977; Mulroy 1971–72; Murray 1981; Palmer 1981; Pöschl 1966; Segal 1981; Springer 1988; Sullivan 1981; Vessey 1985. Gelsomino (1962, 553 n. 1) states his preference for the title "Ode del Soratte," which he believes was coined by Fraenkel (1957), but cf. Cunningham 1964, 35: "the famous Soracte ode (1.9)." The title of chapter 1 of West 1967 is "Horace's Soracte Ode."

37. For a review of the evidence see Nisbet and Hubbard 1970, xlvii–xlviii.

38. Kenney 1970.

by the title "The Soracte Ode." In their sequence, then, the five (very roughly defined) stages of response are Horace's contemporary audience, the late antique and medieval scholiasts, Renaissance and later translators, readers of C. 1.9 as "The Soracte Ode," and the Jaussian reader.

Porphyrio called C. 1.9 *ad Thaliarchum*, and all of the scholiasts' and copyists' titles contain this phrase. It has the obvious function of defining the addressee and thus might seem to show nothing about an ancient response to the poem. On the contrary, as comparison with the title "The Soracte Ode" shows, the title phrase, *ad Thaliarchum*, already reveals a reading of the poem that focuses on the relationship between the speaker (undoubtedly not distinguished from Horace) and the addressee. This focus is all the clearer in the various qualifications of the phrase. For example, in two of the titles *Thaliarchum* is modified by *tiburtium* (R, 1).[39] This adjective gives Thaliarchus a more definite identity and also provides a geographic setting for the poem.[40] The setting is inferred from the first two stanzas, and the author of the title chooses Tibur because of C. 1.7 and other mentions of this region. Likewise, the qualification *puerum speciosum* (b), which assumes a pederastic relationship, is probably inspired by the ode to Ligurinus (C. 4.10) and other indications of pederasty. The scholiastic titles, then, attempt to establish the relationship between Horace and Thaliarchus and to identify certain characteristics of Thaliarchus. The authors of these titles were thus far more alive to the personality of Thaliarchus, as the basis of what the poet says or of his attitude toward Thaliarchus, than are the modern critics who, with "The Soracte Ode," respond to the external references of the poem or to these references as the material of its construction. The moderns ask: what makes C. 1.9 a poem? or, what does the poem mean? The ancients,

---

39. The sigla are those of Hauthal (1966), who reports more variants for pseudo-Acro than does Keller (1967).

40. One group of Horace manuscripts, Klingner's **Q**, has *ad Thaliarchum libertum*. Perhaps *libertum* and *tiburtium* come from the investigations *de personis Horatianis* to which Porphyrio refers (*Sat.* 1.3.21, 90).

trapped in the "intentional fallacy," ask: what was the relationship between Horace and Thaliarchus that inspired C. 1.9?

The scholiastic titles further define the mode of Horace's advice to Thaliarchus as *paranetice* (R, b), one of the several categories of discourse—*erotice, pracmatice, prosphonetice, ypothetice,* and so forth—to which pseudo-Acro assigns the *Odes*. The inventors of the ancient titles, no doubt because of their greater sensitivity to the rhetorical culture in which these poems originated,[41] respond to the fundamental stance of Horace toward his addressee. They hear the poet attempting to win a young man over to a better—for him—way of life. (They do not study Horace creating a poetic work of art.) Thus the first gloss of Porphyrio, his summary of the poem, runs: *Thaliarchum ad laetiorem vitam hortatur, ut lusibus adulescentiae, quamdiu aetas permittat, utatur* ("He exhorts Thaliarchus to a happier life in order that, as long as his age permits, he may enjoy the pleasures of youth."). Porphyrio sums up the poem as a paraenesis in which the period of *adulescentia* has certain prerogatives that Thaliarchus should not neglect. Porphyrio's "reading" is thus at a vast remove both from mine, which responded to the self-concern of the speaker and to the complexities of his advice, and from that of those who call the poem "The Soracte Ode." Further, Porphyrio, who is beyond the horizon of expectations of Horace's original audience, does not see the problematic nature of the advice concerning love, which for him would be simply one of the *lusus adulescentiae*. The same neutrality of response concerning love seems to lie behind the title *Ad taliarchum de voluntatibus*.[42] The author of this title responds to its ethical, paraenetic mode of discourse: Horace is counseling the young man on his desires,[43] which should now be directed toward girls. The term *voluntates* (not, for example, *libidines* or *cupiditates*) suggests an indifference like Porphyrio's to any ethical difficulties.

41. Cf. the remarks in Kenney 1982, 8–9.

42. In the group of manuscripts Klingner designates as Ξ and also given in A (Paris 7900), which Keller takes as the best authority for pseudo-Acro.

43. Most of the ancient titles contain a metrical indication (*tetracolos*), which I have not discussed.

The title "The Soracte Ode" is like the scholiastic titles only in that, not assigned by Horace, it became standard. In other respects, the ancient and modern titles are unlike. The ancient titles supply "factual" information about circumstances of the poem, which, in the scholiasts' conception, are external to it. (For this reason, the metrical indication *tetracolos* often appears paratactically with the other items of information.) Such titles thus stand to the poem as the scholiasts' glosses stand to individual words or phrases. The titles of modern poems, however—and "The Soracte Ode" will be seen to belong to this class—are related to the subject and meaning of the poem.[44] They may be a riddle to which the poem is the answer, or the poem may be a riddle to which the title turns out to be the answer. Part of the "paratext," they are still integral to the reading.[45] So Jauss, too, assumes. Although he does not discuss titles or titling as such, he refers to "the space of expectation awakened by the title word of 'Spleen II.'"[46]

When modern readers called C. 1.9 "The Soracte Ode," they did not choose the simplest, the most obvious, or a somehow inevitable detail from the first stanza for a title. If ease of reference had been the guide, the first three words of the poem would have sufficed, as they do for other odes. "The Soracte Ode" implies that the ode is about Soracte. Yet everyone, including presumably the inventor(s) of this title, knows that the great difficulty of this ode is the transition from the scene depicted in the first stanza to other scenes. Soracte is soon forgotten. Therefore the title refers only to the first

44. Lerner 1983, 199.

45. The term "paratext" is that of G. Genette, who has written in Genette 1988 on the titles of novels. As a few minutes with the MLA International Bibliography on the Wilsondisc CD-ROM show, nearly all of the rather extensive discussion of modern titling concerns novels and short stories. Likewise, research on ancient titling has been mainly on books. For bibliography see Schmalzriedt 1970. See also Kenney 1982, 31–1. Levenston 1978 is the fullest discussion I have found of the function of the titles of modern poems.

46. Jauss 1982, 151.

stanza or perhaps the first two stanzas. And yet, even with this limited reference, the title reflects, and affects, the reading of the whole poem. "The Soracte Ode" assumes Horace's felt, perceptual experience of the mountain, of nature, and those who read the poem under this title assume that this whole poem, like any poem (on their understanding of poetry), must be the expression of emotional experiences of this kind. "The Soracte Ode" thus converts the ode into a modern poem in which the poet's experience is assumed to be the same as the modern, romantic reaction to the sight of a snow-covered mountain.[47]

So strong is the romantic notion of poetry that Soracte alone can somewhat redeem C. 1.9 for those who find it mainly unsuccessful. Eduard Fraenkel's brief, infamous comments on the ode begin: "*Odes I,9, Vides ut alta stet nive candidum Soracte*, is dear to many of us primarily because it reminds us of the days when, either from a *terrazzo* on the roof of one of the tall and weathered houses off the Corso or from the height of the Gianicolo, we gazed at the queer silhouette which the isolated peak of Monte Soratte forms against the northern horizon."[48] Fraenkel here presents two voices. The one that is irrelevant to the present discussion is that of the mundane gentleman scholar who, he lets on, is entertained by (admiring) Roman friends in their houses off the Corso. We are to think of elegant lunches or of aperitifs in the evening on the terrazzo. Never mind that it is, in fact, impossible to see Soracte from "houses off the Corso."[49] The

47. An early record of this kind of response is, unexpectedly, to be found in a letter of Alexander Pope to John Caryll (December 21, 1712): "I shall here put together several beautiful winter pieces of the poets, which have occurred to my memory on this occasion. It may not perhaps be disagreeable to you to compare what lively images nature has presented in different views to some of the greatest geniuses for description which the world ever bred. I shall confine myself to one circumstance only, that of snow." Pope gives examples from Homer and Vergil and then Hor. C. 1.9.1–3. I have the quotation from Goad 1916, 402.

48. Fraenkel 1957, 176.

49. As Daniela Battisti and Robert Wallace independently ascertained for

other voice is that of the romantic enthusiast who "gazes" at Soracte's "queer silhouette." His experience, he believes, must correspond to Horace's, which must be expressed in "The Soracte Ode" (as Fraenkel, too, called it). To that extent (one stanza!), the philologist, yielding to his romanticism, can appreciate the poem.

The tradition of this conflict in criticism between romanticism and philology goes back to Lord Byron, whose well-known parting with Horace took place "upon Soracte's ridge." In the fourth canto of *Childe Harold's Pilgrimage*, the Childe travels from Venice down to Rome.[50] When he reaches the Apennines, he apologizes for his failure to "worship" them more: he has seen the Alps and other great mountains that make "These hills [the Apennines] seem things of lesser dignity" (74.7)—with one exception: "All, save the lone Soracte's height" (74.8). (Byron appears to include Soracte in the Apennines, which may be correct geologically but is incorrect geographically.) Soracte then becomes the occasion for a digression (including a long footnote by the poet) on Horace, Byron's classical education, and his conscious irremediable distance from Horatian, and, by implication, all classical, poetry. The digression begins at the end of the seventy-fourth stanza:

> All, save the lone Soracte's height, displayed
> Not now in snow, which asks the lyric Roman's aid

---

me. It is, of course, possible to see Soracte from certain places on the Gianicolo. Gelsomino (1962, 567–68) admires Fraenkel for having found a way to see Soracte from the Corso!

50. Like C. 1.9, this poem provides the occasion for reflection on titling. It is commonly known as "Childe Harolde," probably because the Childe was immediately assumed to be the author. Byron (1922, 323) complains of this identification at the beginning of the fourth canto in the dedicatory letter to John Hobhouse. This passage also provides the occasion for reflection on the relation of author and speaker in modern as compared with ancient poetry. Consider also that the poem is accompanied by two sets of notes, one by Byron, the other by his traveling companion, John Hobhouse.

75

For our remembrance, and from out the plain
  Heaves like a long-swept wave about to break,
  And on the curl hangs pausing: not in vain
  May he, who will, his recollections rake,
  And quote in classic raptures, and awake
  The hills with Latian echoes—I abhorred
  Too much, to conquer for the Poet's sake,[51]
  The drilled dull lesson, forced down word by word
In my repugnant youth, with pleasure to record

76

Aught that recalls the daily drug which turned
  My sickening memory;[52] and, though Time hath taught
  My mind to meditate what then it learned,
  Yet such the fixed inveteracy wrought
  By the impatience of my early thought,
  That, with the freshness wearing out before
  My mind could relish what it might have sought,
  If free to choose, I cannot now restore
Its health—but what it then detested, still abhor.

77

Then farewell, Horace—whom I hated so,
  Not for thy faults, but mine: it is a curse
  To understand, not feel thy lyric flow,
  To comprehend but never love thy verse;
  Although no deeper Moralist rehearse

51. Byron's footnote is marked here.
52. Is 75.6 ("I abhorred")–76.2 ("sickening memory") a malicious parody in English of Horatian syntax? I construe the first infinitive construction ("to conquer") as depending on "The drilled dull lesson." ("[T]o conquer" = to be conquered.) The whole phrase ("to conquer for the Poet's sake") is thus tantamount to a gerundive modifying "lesson." The second infinitive construction ("with pleasure to record") follows from "Too much."

Our little life, nor Bard prescribe his art,
Nor livelier Satirist the conscience pierce,
Awakening without wounding the touched heart,
Yet fare thee well—upon Soracte's ridge we part.

The movement of thought in this digression begins and ends with Soracte. The Childe begins by contrasting himself with someone who, inspired to "classic raptures" by Soracte, might quote C. 1.9; the Childe never learned enough Latin for that. He goes on to express his regret about his classical education in the next two stanzas, and Byron adds a long footnote.[53] What is it in Horace that the Childe believes he has lost? In the footnote, Byron explains in a series of antitheses his early failure to appreciate Horace: "I wish to express, that we become tired of the task [of learning Greek and Latin] before we can comprehend the beauty; that we learn by rote before we can get by heart [note that in Byron's usage 'to get by heart' is the opposite of memorization]; that freshness is worn away, and the future pleasure and advantage deadened, by the didactic anticipation, at an age when we can neither feel nor understand the power of compositions which it requires an acquaintance with life, as well as Latin and Greek, to relish, or to reason upon."[54] The principal antitheses, which have reappeared thousands of times in various forms since Byron's day, are:

Negative	Positive
fatigue	comprehend beauty
memorization (cf. 76.2)	get by heart
pedagogy (cf. 75.8)	freshness (cf. 76.6)
Greek and Latin	life.

The Childe's loss, as he sees it, is the beauty that he would have found in Horace, the emotional experience of that beauty that he might have had. Note that Horace is for him the "lyric Roman" (74.9); that he

---

53. In Byron 1922, the footnote is thirty-four lines long.
54. Byron 1922, 386–87.

seems especially to regret his failure to appreciate Horace's lyrics, which he can distinguish from the *Satires* and the *Ars Poetica* (77). In particular, he regrets that he can only "understand, not feel" the lyrics (77.3). As for Soracte, then, the Childe's present enraptured experience of it makes up for the poetic experience of it that he believes he might have had in reading Horace if he had not been forced to read him at such an early age. He assumes that Horace has expressed something about Soracte that corresponds to his own present experience. Thus the Childe can imagine "classic raptures," that is, the raptures that are expressed in classical lyric and experienced (note "not in vain," 75.3) by those who both understand and feel the expression. Soracte is thus a bridge between a present felt experience and a past experience *manqué*. The Childe bids a fond farewell to Horace and concludes, "upon Soracte's ridge we part." But no such parting can take place because no such meeting can take place. Horace would never have set foot on Soracte either literally or figuratively, and his reaction to the sight of the mountain was in every way unlike the Childe's or Byron's. Horace can appear on Soracte's ridge only in the romantic imagination, the same imagination that produced "The Soracte Ode" as a title of C. 1.9.[55]

55. The influence of Byron on the title is, I suppose, indirect. As Wendell Clausen has pointed out to me, the diary kept by Nathaniel Hawthorne during his visit to Italy in 1858 provides an example of the direct influence of Byron on the perception of Soracte. When he first describes the mountain, Hawthorne refers to Byron's description (Hawthorne 1980, 233–34). In a second description, Hawthorne again shows the influence of Byron: "Walking on a little further, Soracte came fully into view, starting with bold abruptness out of the middle of the country; and before we got back, the bright Italian moon was throwing a shower of silver over the scene and making it so beautiful it seems miserable not to know how to put it into words; a foolish thought, however, for such scenes are an expression in themselves, and were never meant to be translated into any language" (Hawthorne 1980, 236). Hawthorne has experienced the same ineffable raptures. Hawthorne sometimes refers to a guidebook published by the firm of John Murray and Son, *A Handbook for Travellers in Central Italy, including the Papal States, Rome, and the Cities of Etruria* (Lon-

Four Translations of Odes 1.9

From the rediscovery of the odes in the Renaissance up until the nineteenth century, the only record of reader response to C. 1.9, aside from occasional, too brief departures from conjecture and gloss, is translation.[56] Bentley's edition of Horace (1711) immediately comes to mind as a possible source for a great scholar's response. His commentary on C. 1.9 is indeed a response, but not that of a reader to the poem. His response is more often directed at other scholars, and *adversaria*, the usual term for his remarks, is fitting.[57] To translations, then, one turns, of which four will be discussed here. The first is that of Henry Rider (1638), the earliest English translation I found;[58] the second is that of John Dryden (1685); the third is that of William Cowper (ca. 1782); and the fourth is that of the classicist, John Conington (1863).

Each of these translations is studied as the translator's response to C. 1.9 cast in the poetic idiom of his own day.[59] This new poem, it is assumed, is the translator's answer to a new question concerning

---

don, 1843). The editor of the diary points out that, apropos of Soracte, the Murray handbook quoted stanzas 74–75 of the fourth canto of *Childe Harold's Pilgrimmage* (Hawthorne 1980, 795). One can surmise that Byron's perceptions of Italy became to some extent normative for subsequent romantic travelers.

56. Bolgar 1964 does not list translations of the *Odes* into English. See Lathrop 1933 and Palmer 1911 for lists of translations.

57. Cf. Shackleton Bailey 1982, 111: "To read these notes, *even when they do not extort at least temporary assent,* is one of the most stimulating experiences in Latin scholarship" (my emphasis).

58. Translations of selected odes were published before 1638. See Pollard and Redgrave 1986, s.v. Horatius Flaccus, Quintus. I have not checked these earlier translations and do not know if they include C. 1.9.

59. See Cook 1986 for a survey of the views of Walter Benjamin, Maurice Blanchot, Jacques Derrida, Hans-Georg Gadamer, and Jean-Paul Sartre on translation. Cook concludes: "If translation has been seen as a transformation of the text, it can only be because the notion of translation already includes, in this understanding of it, that of reading" (148).

Horace's poem, a question different both from the one Horace's original audience would have asked and from the ones guiding my hermeneutic reading. The paratext accompanying Rider's, Dryden's, and
Conington's translations helps to define the questions they asked of
Horace. Unfortunately, we have no way of knowing how the first two
translators were influenced by the paratext of C. 1.9 in their editions
of Horace. From Rider's short dedicatory preface, we can see that he
had read commentary on the odes, perhaps in the form of scholia in
his edition of Horace. We do not know what edition it was. As for
Dryden, it is known that in translating from Latin he often used Latin
prose summaries of poems and other material he found in his editions. As in the case of Rider, we do not know what edition of Horace
he used. Conington refers to the commentaries of Orelli and Ritter,
of which he preferred the former's.[60]

   The goal, then, of this approach to these translations is not criticism of their aesthetic merits or of their effectiveness in rendering
meanings that I or others have found in the Latin text. Rather, this
approach focuses on the differences between the translator's reading,
inferred from his new poem, and that of other readers before him
and after him.

The Translation of Henry Rider (1638)[61]

Ode IX

To Thaliarchus

The sharper the winter is, the sweeter our mirth should be.

Seest thou Soracte white with a deepe snow?
How the bow'd trees their weight can't undergoe?

---

60. See Bottkol 1943, 399–404, for Dryden's reliance on the paratext of the
Latin text; Conington 1863, xxx.

61. I have used here the 1644 reprint, the text of which is identical to that
of the 1638 edition. See Pollard and Redgrave 1986, s.v. Horatius Flaccus, Quintus, no. 13804.

And how the streames bound with sharpe ice, doe stand?
Dissolve the frost, laying with bounteous hand   4
Wood on the fire, and with a courage bold
Draw, Thaliarch, thy wine of foure yeares old,
Out of thy Sabine two-ear'd pot: the rest
Leave to the gods, who when they have supprest   8
The winds on the rude sea maintaining warre,
Nor Cypres, nor old Ash-trees shaken are.
"Enquire thou not what shall to morrow bee,
"And whatsoere day fortune giveth thee,   12
"Put it upon thy gaines; nor sweet love-glances
Doe thou abhore, O boy, nor yet our dance.
While crabbed age forbeare thy youth a space,
Let both the martiall field and wrestling place,   16
And softly-whispers when the night comes in,
At a fit season be reviv'd agin;
And the maids pleasant laugh that her betraid
Within some private corner closely laid,   20
Or favour being snatched from her arme
Or finger having done some trifling harme.

This version of C. 1.9 comes from the first complete translation
of the odes of Horace in English, which Rider dedicated to Robert,
Lord Rich. Horace, Rider reminds his patron, "was as meanly de-
scended as my own selfe; yet did not his meanness deprive him of a
presidiairie *Maecenas*, a Roman Knight, high in Honours, and (which
was the greatest) in his Prince's love." No doubt Lord Rich's expectations influenced Rider's work: the translation answered the question concerning Horace that Rider assumed Lord Rich would ask.
From the paratext of the translation of C. 1.9, it is already clear how
Rider proposed to read the ode. The title "To Thaliarchus" would
probably have been in Rider's edition; the brief summary may also
have been.[62] Title and summary are not unrelated. As I have already

62. In Fea 1827 I find the subtitle: *Quo magis saevit hiems, eo magis voluptati in-
dulgendum.*

said, this form of the title, in contrast with "The Soracte Ode," assumes that the hortatory stance of the speaker toward Thaliarchus is the essential thing. Rider's summary then gives the gist of the speaker's advice: "The sharper the winter is, the sweeter our mirth should be." The speaker is not advising Thaliarchus to change his principles and way of life; rather, Thaliarchus should, with the material and spiritual resources he already has, maintain a cheerful disposition despite the adverse weather. Having found this moral in the ode, Rider must accommodate stanzas 4 to 6 of the original to the fireside setting of the opening in such a way that warm weather and love are not changes to which Thaliarchus should look forward but past experiences the recollection of which should improve his mood. Thus *repetantur* becomes "reviv'd agin" (18), and the past tense is used for the encounter with the girl ("betraid," "laid," 19–20). The theme of youth and age is diminished as the speaker becomes Thaliarchus' coeval: the dance is "our dance" (14).

Different readers will respond differently to the tone of the speaker. For Rider, he is moralistic. Thus *benignius* is exaggerated into "with a courage bold" (5), and the chiding second person singular attaches to both wine and pot—"thy wine" (6), "thy . . . pot" (7). This use of the possessive, not recognized in twentieth-century dictionaries of American or English, could be called the ethical genitive. Dr. Johnson's third of three definitions of "thy" approaches the sense but is too general: "relating to thee." One of his examples, however, from Cowley (without further reference), is exactly analogous to Rider's usage: "Whatever God did say, / Is all thy clear and smooth uninterrupted way." Here "thy" clearly means: the way you should take, in obedience to God. Rider's "thy" is of the same sort. His fondness for the moralistic is also shown in his practice of picking out maxims with quotation marks (11–13).[63] In sum, Rider has asked of C. 1.9: what useful moral does it contain? Having decided, as in the summary

---

63. For example, he sets off C. 1.3.25–26 (*Audax omnia perpeti / gens humana,* etc.) and C. 1.4.13–14 (*Pallida mors aequo pulsat pede,* etc.) with quotation marks.

placed at the head of the translation, what the moral is, Rider then
consistently renders the Latin in such a way as to express that moral.

The Translation of John Dryden (1685)[64]

Horace

The Ninth Ode of the First Book

I

Behold yon mountain's hoary height,
    Made higher with new mounts of snow;
Again behold the winter's weight
    Oppress the labouring woods below:
And streams, with icy fetters bound,   5
Benumb'd and crampt to solid ground.

II

With well-heap'd logs dissolve the cold,
    And feed the genial hearth with fires;
Produce the wine, that makes us bold,
    And sprightly wit and love inspires: 10
For what hereafter shall betide,
God, if 'tis worth his care, provide.

III

Let him alone, with what he made,
    To toss and turn the world below;
At his command the storms invade;   15
    The winds by his commission blow;
Till with a nod he bids 'em cease,
And then the calm returns, and all is peace.

---

64. From *The Poetical Works of John Dryden*, ed. Joseph and John Warton et al.
(London 1811), 2:584–86. Dryden 1909, which I have used for Dryden's preface to the collection in which his translation of *C.* 1.9 appeared, modernizes
spellings in the text of the translation and removes contracted forms.

IV

To-morrow and her works defy,
   Lay hold upon the present hour,   20
And snatch the pleasures passing by,
To put them out of fortune's power:
Nor love, nor love's delights disdain;
Whate'er thou get'st to-day, is gain.

V

Secure those golden early joys,   25
   That youth unsour'd with sorrow bears,
Ere withering time the taste destroys,
   With sickness and unwieldy years.
For active sports, for pleasing rest,
This is the time to be possest;   30
The best is but in season best.

VI

The appointed hour of promis'd bliss,
   The pleasing whisper in the dark,
The half unwilling willing kiss,
   The laugh that guides thee to the mark,   35
When the kind nymph would coyness feign,
And hides but to be found again;
These, these are joys, the gods for youth ordain.

Dryden's title is as neutral as possible. His translation comes with abundant paratext, however, in the form of his preface to the collection in which it appeared, *Sylvae, or The second Part of Poetical Miscellanies*. Dryden was what we would now call a contributing editor of this collection, although he had not, he says, read some of its contents.[65] Of the translations he here published, four were from Horace, three odes (C. 1.3, 9; 3.29) and the third *Epode*. Of the three odes, two carry dedications, and, in the preface, Dryden expatiates on one of

---

65. Dryden 1909, 181, col. 2.

them. The choice of C. 1.9 is left unexplained, and Dryden says nothing about this particular ode. Dryden's general remarks about Horace are useful, however. He divided the odes into three categories, the panegyrical, the moral, and the "jovial, or (if I may so call them) Bacchanalian."[66] He must have placed C. 1.9 in either the second or the third category but it is hard to say in which. Dryden's Horace is above all doctrinaire. If Rider's was moralistic, Dryden's is moralizing. Horace's indicative *Vides* immediately becomes the imperative, "Behold." The doctrine that Dryden's Horace expounds is Epicureanism, which, Dryden was convinced, was Horace's philosophy: "His morals are uniform . . . for, let his Dutch commentators say what they will, his philosophy was Epicurean; and he made use of gods and providence only to serve a turn in poetry."[67]

Dryden thus, while he converts the gods of stanza 3 into "God," in apparent conformity with Christian belief, creates an otiose ("if 'tis worth his care," 12) and distant ("Let him alone," 13) divinity who could join Lucretius' gods in the *intermundia*. This "God" can easily coexist with "the gods"—harmless classicizing—of the last stanza (38). In proper Epicurean fashion, the power of chance is denied: pleasures are snatched away from fortune (21–22), whereas in Horace fortune is the giver of the days of human life.

Dryden explicitly distinguished between the philosophical and the poetical, however,[68] and he was acutely sensitive to the styles of the ancient poets he translated in *Sylvae* (Vergil, Lucretius, and Theocritus in addition to Horace). In my opinion, he is a fine critic. As for his translations, he seems to have decided in advance which particular qualities of each poet he would attempt to convey in English. In the case of Horace, he said, "the most distinguishing part of all his character seems to me to be his briskness, his jollity, and his good humor; and those I have chiefly endeavor'd to copy."[69] But briskness

66. Dryden 1909, 181, col. 1.
67. Dryden 1909, 180, col. 2.
68. Dryden 1909, 180, col. 1.
69. Dryden 1909, 181, col. 1.

is hardly a trait of Dryden's translation of C. 1.9. Dryden takes thirty-eight lines to translate Horace's twenty-four, increasing the length of the original by more than half.

With briskness, jollity and good humor are lost, too. Dryden is determined to draw out antitheses that Horace left implicit. In the first stanza, for example, Dryden stresses the "height" of Soracte, "made higher" by the snow. To the height of the mountain is opposed the level of the woods "below," and then, at a third, lower level, the rivers are, by hyperbole, "solid ground" (6). The antithesis between mountain and woods is intensified by the anaphora of "Behold . . . / Again behold. . . ." Dryden's desire—and ability—to pack rhetorical and, as he must have felt, Latinate features into the translation, to go Horace one better, as it were, is thus on display from the beginning. While Horace is content to describe the snow-covered Soracte in seven words, Dryden uses twelve, because he wants to deploy a chiasmus not found in the original:

A   B
mountain's hoary height,
        B   A
Made higher with new mounts of snow.

Alliteration reinforces the chiasmus.

Dryden's instinct for elaboration is observable from beginning to end of the translation. The result is a dense rhetorical surface and, simultaneously, the loss of the more fundamental rhetorical situation of the original, the stance of a particular speaker toward a particular addressee. Dryden does not name Thaliarchus or any addressee. Dryden's speaker addresses an anonymous audience, expounding a doctrine of pleasure or, more precisely, of love. Love enters already in the second stanza (10). The original's rather abrupt introduction of the theme in the fourth stanza is of no interest to Dryden. Horace's metaphor of gain now applies to love (23–24), not to the days of one's life. Dryden eliminates the tryst from the next-to-last stanza, in such a way that the theme of love reaches a distinct conclusion in the last stanza. (The next-to-last stanza is left to conclude with a maxim—

"The best is but in season best," 31.) In order to give weight to the conclusion, he increases each of the last two stanzas by a line, making a triple rhyme (ABABCCC), and the very last line is increased by an extra foot—perhaps the clearest example of Dryden's technique of amplification.

Sensitive as Dryden undoubtedly was to the manner of Horace, exigencies—most of which it is beyond me to explain—caused him to put C. 1.9 into an English that seems to strive for remoteness from the original. But this remoteness is a clue to Dryden's reading of C. 1.9. Dryden must have attempted to answer the question: what was the creed that inspired verse of this quality? Dryden must have felt that the excellence of the verse was a proof of the creed. The translation should put this creed across in the new language, and, since it was only implicit in the original, the translation would have to amplify it. The translation of C. 1.9 thus became a rhetorically embellished sermon on love.

The Translation of William Cowper (ca. 1782)[70]

See'st thou yon mountain laden with deep snow,
The groves beneath their fleecy burthen bow,
   The streams congeal'd forget to flow;
Come, thaw the cold, and lay a cheerful pile
     Of fuel on the hearth;   5
Broach the best cask, and make old Winter smile
     With seasonable mirth.

This be our part—let heaven dispose the rest;
     If Jove command, the winds shall sleep,

70. Cowper 1926, 529. This reference is to Milford's edition, which was revised by Kenneth Povey and N. H. Russell (1971). This new edition, which I was unable to obtain, contains a note dating the translation to "before 1782." John D. Baird has pointed out to me that in the 1815 edition by John Johnson, the poet's relative, the translation of C. 1.9 is placed after a poem dated 1789 in a sequence broadly chronological. I have accepted Baird's suggestion that the more cautious "about 1782" be used.

That now wage war upon the foamy deep,   10
And gentle gales spring from the balmy west.
   E'en let us shift to-morrow as we may,
     When to-morrow's past away,
     We at least shall have to say,
     We have liv'd another day;   15
Your auburn locks will soon be silver'd o'er,
Old age is at our heels, and youth returns no more.

Conington, whose translation of C. 1.9 is discussed after Cowper's, complained that "men of great original gifts" no longer translated Horace, and indeed Cowper had been the last English poet of any note to attempt to put C. 1.9 into his own language. Cowper's translation, notable for its omission of lines 15–16 and 18–24 of the original, suggests that C. 1.9 had become in one respect unreadable. The speaker's practical advice to Thaliarchus concerning springtime trysts could no longer be accommodated to the winter setting. The poem fell into two halves, of which one had to be omitted. The problem of the two "halves" of the poem that was to beset philology for so many years was already at hand. Cowper also anticipated the sensibility of a Walter Savage Landor (1775–1864), who, in his copy of Horace, sometimes struck out the last stanzas of the odes, writing negative comments in the margins.[71]

Cowper's new poem is in two stanzas, of which the first corresponds to C. 1.9.1–8 (stanzas 1 and 2) and the second to C. 1.9.9–15 and 17–18 (stanza 3 and parts of stanzas 4 and 5). Versification (variation in line lengths) and rhyme (triple and quadruple) suggest a song. In each of his stanzas, Cowper has worked a reversal of the mood of the corresponding parts of the original. He has made the winter scene as attractive as possible. While the notion of season was only implicit in C. 1.9, in Cowper's translation winter is personified and has the endearing epithet "old" (6). While the scene was bleak in Horace, it is unforbidding in Cowper: the snow on the trees is a

---

71. Highet 1957, 122, reporting a finding of Archibald Y. Campbell.

"fleecy burthen" (2) and the rivers are not frozen with sharp ice—
they "forget to flow" (3). Indeed, the mood is one of good cheer and
mirth. One of Cowper's means of working this transformation is gen-
eralization. Soracte has become "yon mountain" (1). Thaliarchus is
not named; the addressee has no discernible characteristics in the first
stanza. The wine of C. 1.9 has become simply "the best cask" (6). Both
the Greek and the Roman aspects of the wine have disappeared. The
ordinariness of Horace's wine has been optimized, like everything
else in C. 1.9. What Nisbet and Hubbard said of the first stanza of C.
1.9—that it is a Christmas card—is still truer of Cowper's first stanza.
Santa Claus and his reindeer would not be obtrusive.

   Horace's or his speaker's advice to Thaliarchus in stanzas 4 to
6 is positive: Thaliarchus should undertake various pleasant activities
appropriate to his youthful years. Cowper's speaker, by contrast, is
completely resigned. Cowper's second stanza begins, "This be our
part" (8), referring to the pleasures of the winter's day and thereto
restricting his and his companion's scope of concern. The storm at
sea (third stanza of C. 1.9) becomes simultaneous with the winter
scene: "the winds . . . / That now . . ." (9–10; my emphasis). Cowper
again, as in his implicit division of C. 1.9 into two halves, anticipates
a future problem of reception, providing a kind of unity that some
philologists would later require. Cowper's storm at sea is as benign,
at least potentially, as the cold winter's day. Expect "gentle gales"
from the "balmy west" (11). Not only should we be resigned to this
day, we should be resigned to whatever happens tomorrow (12). At
this point, Cowper changes Horace's thought radically. Whereas Horace spoke of the number of days of life vouchsafed by fortune, Cowper speaks of the quality of each successive day ("E'en let us shift tomorrow as we may," 12). We do not count each day in and of itself
as gain, as in Horace. We first factor out the particular quality of each
day and then accept the day even if it was unpleasant. With Cowper,
we become connoisseurs of our fortune. Cowper strangely concludes
with the notion of irretrievable youth as an argument for the resignation that he has counseled, in effect reversing the argument of the
speaker in C. 1.9. Whereas the speaker used this notion to encourage

Thaliarchus to capitalize on the days of youth, Cowper uses youth to encourage his addressee to be passive. Cowper was obviously determined to keep the thought of *donec virenti canities abest / morosa* (C. 1.9.17–18: "as long as peevish, hoary age is removed from your green youth") at whatever cost to logic.

This peculiarity of the translation and also the larger omission of the second "half" of the original can be explained, I believe, with reference to the dramatic situation that Cowper has imagined (though not effectively integrated in his new poem). Whereas the first stanza, in which the speaker addresses a second person, seems to reflect the dramatic structure of C. 1.9, the second stanza begins with a first person plural pronoun: "This be *our* part" (8; my emphasis). In the counsel of resignation, set apart by rhyme (quadruple), line length, and, visually, by indentation, "we" is stressed by position, by anaphora, and by meter (with syncopation of the first element of the first iamb) (14–15). In the last line, old age is "at *our* heels" (my emphasis). The speaker and the addressee are the same age. The speaker's counsel is for both of them equally. It does not arise from the speaker's greater and different experience. The only difference between speaker and addressee in the second stanza appears in the next-to-last line: "*Your* auburn locks . . ." (16; my emphasis). This one slight distinction between himself and the addressee would make sense if the speaker were a man and the addressee were a woman (let us say, his wife). On this understanding of the relationship, it also becomes clear why the Horatian speaker's advice about pursuing girls could not come into the translation.

The Translation of John Conington (1863)

Ode IX

Vides ut alta.

See, how it stands, one pile of snow,
    Soracte! 'neath the pressure yield
Its groaning woods; the torrents' flow

With clear sharp ice is all congeal'd.
Heap high the logs, and melt the cold,   5
   Good Thaliarch; draw the wine we ask,
That mellower vintage, four-year-old,
   From out the cellar'd Sabine cask.
The future trust with Jove; when He
   Has still'd the warring tempests' roar   10
On the vex'd deep, the cypress-tree
   And aged ash are rock'd no more.
O, ask not what the morn will bring,
   But count as gain each day that chance
May give you; sport in life's young spring,   15
   Nor scorn sweet love, nor merry dance,
While years are green, while sullen eld
   Is distant. Now the walk, the game,
The whisper'd talk at sunset held,
   Each in its hour, prefer their claim.   20
Sweet too the laugh, whose feign'd alarm
   The hiding-place of beauty tells,
The token, ravish'd from the arm
   Or finger, that but ill rebels.

Conington (1825–69) was the Corpus Professor of Latin at Oxford University. In a lengthy introduction to his translation of the *Odes*, he explains the conditions he had laid down for himself. As for versification, he demanded "metrical conformity" to the original. Rhyme was for pleasure, he apologized, but the alternate rhymes of his translation gave the effect of the four-line Horatian stanza.[72] Indeed, Conington's translation of C. 1.9 not only preserves this effect but clearly even intends to render the Latin line for line, preserving as many features of syntax and word order as possible. For example, the sentence end after *morosa* in line 18 is matched in the same line of the translation ("Is distant"). Another example of matching syntax

72. Conington 1863, vi and ix.

is the subordinate clause beginning at the next-to-last word in line 9 ("when He"). Compare *qui simul* in the same line in the original. C. 1.9.21–22 inevitably defeated Conington, but in lines 23–24, as in a surprising number of other places, he was able to capture the word order of the original exactly.

Conington's specular tour de force constantly invites comparison with the Latin of C. 1.9. The reader of this translation must either know C. 1.9 by heart or have the text before him. A Latin-less reader could never appreciate Conington's reading of the Latin, for it is devoted to technical and stylistic matters. For the very reason that it keeps so close to the original, Conington's translation reveals his prejudices at the one point at which he changes the sense of the Latin. Horace's *composita . . . hora* (20) ("at an appointed hour") becomes "Each in its hour," referring to all of the activities recommended to Thaliarchus by the speaker. But in Horace the phrase refers only to the tryst, as the speaker proceeds to concentrate on love as the most enticing of youth's pleasures. Conington betrays in his translation a certain moral disapproval of Horace that is quite explicit in his introduction.

While Conington admired the so-called Roman odes of book 3, some of the other odes were morally repugnant,[73] and all of them were dull:

> The Odes of Horace . . . will, I think, strike a reader who comes back to them after reading other books as distinguished by a simplicity, monotony, and almost poverty of sentiment, and as depending for the charm of their external form not so much on novel and ingenious images as on musical words aptly chosen and aptly combined. We are always hearing of wine-jars and Thracian convivialities, of parsley wreaths and Syrian nard; the graver topics, which it is the poet's wisdom to forget, are constantly typified by the terrors of quivered Medes and painted Gelonians; there is the perpetual antithesis between youth and age,

73. Conington 1863, xvi–xxxi.

there is the ever-recurring image of green and withered trees, and it is only the attractiveness of the Latin, half real, half perhaps arising from association and the romance of a language not one's own, that make us feel this "lyrical common-place" more supportable than common-place is usually found to be.[74]

This condemnation obviously has C. 1.9 in particular in mind. All that is left for the translator is "to reproduce beauties depending on expression." But the appropriate English diction would be that of the eighteenth century. The translator must not reflect his own time: "I believe that the chief danger which a translator has to avoid is that of subjection to the influences of his own period."[75]

The superficial closeness of Conington's translation to its original is thus based on a profound estrangement. C. 1.9 can no longer be the answer to a new question for a new reading that will yield a new translation. Conington's translation is new only in the sense that, when it is published, it is historically the latest in the sequence of such translations. Conington is not alone, however, in his inability to read Horace. Though Byron believed that his early education was to blame for his insensitivity to Horace, the real reason was a historical change in taste and sentiment, of which Byron himself was a notable representative. Another was Goethe, whose judgment on Horace's odes was exactly the same as the one that Conington later expressed: "the poetic talent of Horace can be recognized only in his aiming at technical and linguistic perfection, i.e. imitation of Greek meters and poetic language, beside a fearful reality devoid of all real poetry, especially in the odes."[76]

74. Conington 1863, xxvi–xxvii.
75. Conington 1863, xxvii–xxviii, xxvi.
76. Quoted in Teuffel 1920, 66.

2

. . . .

Other
Approaches

4

· · · · · · · · · · · ·

Scholarship

A survey of the scholarship usually comes at the beginning of an article or a book. The scholar defines the state of the question and points to omissions and/or errors in the literature, thereby opening the way for his or her new contribution. The discussion of C. 1.9 in the preceding chapters was not intended, however, primarily as a contribution to scholarship but as the testing of a method for, or an approach to, the reading of this ode. In chapter 1, a first reading was attempted that even suppressed philology to the extent possible. In chapters 2 and 3, both my own research and other scholars' findings came into play, but within the horizon of the first reading. The principle or starting point of the approach was the poem as an aesthetic object (as distinguished, for example, from a text for commentary or a text containing "problems" as defined by previous scholarship). My approach therefore at least implicitly called into question the relation between philology and hermeneutical reading. Accordingly, the brief survey of the scholarship on C. 1.9 in this chapter will explicitly concentrate on philology's manner of dealing with the poem as an aesthetic object.

But philology's concern is not only aesthetic. The aesthetic character of a work is only half, so to speak, of philology's business. At a 1981 conference on literary hermeneutics and the interpretation of classical texts, a spokesman for philology introduced his remarks on C. 1.9, to which several papers were devoted,[1] in this way: "The philologist's goal . . . is first to *explain* a particular poem by setting it in its literary, social, historical, and linguistic contexts; then, secondly, as a critic, to throw light on its aesthetic value, if possible, by a variety of strategies, perhaps by defending its 'consistency.' "[2] Philology's procedure is thus divided into two parts, and the two have a determined sequence: first, the philological-historical explanation of contexts, and, second, aesthetic understanding. This sequence is exactly the opposite of the one followed in the Jaussian reading of C. 1.9. The survey of the scholarship on this ode will therefore have to observe not only aesthetic arguments and conclusions but also, and more intently, the manner in which the primary philological and historical investigations are related to the secondary aesthetic enterprise.

For the aesthetic side of philological investigation, the ode's unity has long been the main concern.[3] Over a century of scholarship divides into two main notions of unity, both of which are contained in August Boeckh's canonical statement on the unity of the work of literary art: "Wherein lies the unity of the work of art? It consists principally in the unity of the object that is represented in the work. As Pheidias had in his mind, as the basic thought and unity of Olympian Zeus, the undivided inner intuition of that which was externally represented, the individuality of Zeus himself in his essence, so every verbal work of art is related to a content delimited as a unity." This objective unity is linked to a subjective unity, a unity of thought, by the purpose of the work. For the determination of unity, everything depends on the discovery of the purpose, or of what we would call

---

1. The hermeneutical papers on C. 1.9 (Murray 1981; Palmer 1981), despite the title of the conference, applied a philosophical hermeneutics to the poem and discovered in it what Heidegger had said was true of art in general. These papers, lacking a specifically literary hermeneutics, tend to be allegorical in their reading. Nevertheless, some of their general observations are relevant to the present chapter. See Palmer 1981, 294–95.

2. Sullivan 1981, 277.

3. Cf. Plüss 1882, 65.

"authorial intention." Boeckh explains how to find the purpose of the work through analysis, through comparison of its parts and through investigation of its construction.[4] Boeckh's two kinds of unity, objective and subjective, are the same ones that turn up in scholarship on C. 1.9. His use of an analogy from plastic art, Pheidias' Zeus, has more subtle implications, however. For, as will be seen, especially subjective unity tends to be stated in visual terms, or at least in metaphors.

Both kinds of unity were first argued for in reaction against the notion of Horace as slavish imitator of Alcaeus, of C. 1.9 as a practice piece in which Horace was learning to free himself from his Greek model.[5] The reduction of the poem to an imitation entailed the denial of its unity, even when Horace's own original traits were acknowledged, as in the notorious condemnation of C. 1.9 by Wilamowitz: "it is of course a pastiche, a groping experiment, so that the Thracian rivers, which are frozen, have come to a standstill beside the snow covered peak of Soracte, which can send its gleam across to us, too, as to Horace, on the Esquiline. The admonition to the boy, who also gets the wine—thus must be a servant—and goes out into Rome for amatory adventures, unites equally contradictory features; the best are not at all taken from Alcaeus. Pretty verses but still not a poem."[6] Such a criticism could be met by showing that the frozen rivers did not necessarily come from Alcaeus: Horace could have seen them with his own eyes. Nohl replied to Wilamowitz with a quotation from the *Lebenserinnerungen* of Ludwig Richter, who had seen the Tiber cov-

4. Boeckh 1886, 131–32 (quotation p. 131), 144, 149–55. Though published in 1886, this work is based on lectures that Boeckh began to give in 1809. Rudd 1960, 373 n. 1, gives a short bibliography of works on the problem of the unity of the Horatian ode.

5. Arnold 1891, 87.

6. Wilamowitz 1913, 311. Observe that the form of criticism is the same as in Fraenkel (quoted above in chapter 3). The critic establishes his authority by reference to his own experience in Rome: because I have seen Soracte from the Esquiline, that must be Horace's vantage point in this poem. Wilamowitz's witticism about the Thracian rivers in Italy is already in Kiessling 1881, 62.

ered with a thin rind of ice. But the "rivers" of C. 1.9.4 need not refer
to the Tiber: "As his fantasy was perhaps stimulated by the trees in
Maecenas' park on the Esquiline to the *silvae laborantes*, which in reality
he did not see, so the crust of ice in a wagon track could have caused
him to see the *flumina consistentia*."[7] Nohl concludes that Horace's description is not derivative but comes from his real experience (*wirklich
Erlebte*) and that his description of the winter landscape is thus more
unified than Alcaeus'. An objective unity has been found.

Giorgio Pasquali, repeating Nohl's conclusion concerning stanza
1, argues the same case more fully. Again, the scene comes from lived
experience (*vita vissuta*). Pasquali then goes on to discuss the rest of
the poem. Though his main concern, in keeping with the central argument of his book as a whole, is not the poem's unity but its Hellenistic (and therefore non-Alcaic) or "Hellenistic-Roman" character,
he also provides an account of the organization of the poem.[8] Curiously, the unity that Pasquali finds is not objective, not based on lived
experience, as the title of his chapter on C. 1.9 ("The Winter Ode")
might have led one to expect, but on the metaphoric character of the
first stanza. The unity of C. 1.9 is thus, in Boeckh's terms, and con-
formably to Boeckh's canon, also subjective. Pasquali writes:

> For Horace, winter and snow, as Kiessling has already observed
> [Kiessling 1881], are not only natural events but also internal facts,
> states of mind. Winter weighs on his soul, snow falls on his soul.
> Only one who understands thus will succeed in feeling—be-
> cause understanding in the abstract is of no use—the movement
> to *permitte divis cetera*. "Yesterday the storm raged on land and sea.
> Today the fields lie peacefully beneath the snow. The air is over-
> cast but calm. What will happen tomorrow? It's useless to ask.
> Live and love." But living and loving for Horace are incarnated
> in joyful games of young lovers in the warm air of spring. The
> poet, while he sits by the fire, paints for himself, in imagination,

7. Nohl 1915, 21–22.
8. Pasquali 1920, 78–79, 86.

the joys of the time when it will be possible to spend the day outdoors. The sentiment of the stanza [that is, the third stanza] explains the allusion to the sea that was raging yesterday: today it's calm. Often when Horace thinks of a turbid and stormy soul, the image of the sea appears to him. Should one suppose that, when he sang *ut melius, quidquid erit pati, seu pluris hiemes seu tribuit Iuppiter ultimam, quae oppositis debilitat pumicibus mare Tyrrhenum* [C. 1.11.3–6], he was with Leuconoe on the shore of the ocean?[9]

Pasquali thus describes the subjective unity, the unity of thought, of the poem, which begins with the metaphorical aspect of the winter scene that Pasquali began by describing as "lived experience." Of course, the scene could be both "real" and metaphorical.[10]

Pasquali was one of the few to discover both kinds of unity in C. 1.9. His successors tend to argue for one or the other, often in the belief that one excludes the other. If the poem is based on—if its unity depends on—real experience, it cannot be symbolic. If the poem contains symbolism—if its unity depends thereon—then real experience does not have to be considered. The latter school of thought did not emerge until twenty-five years after Pasquali, with a few remarks by L. P. Wilkinson,[11] though it had ancestors in Kiessling, cited by Pasquali, and in German scholars before Kiessling.[12] Indeed, little interpretation of any kind appeared until after World War II.[13] The publication of Eduard Fraenkel's *Horace* in 1957 was a turning point. In the period of the New Criticism came a series of articles and an important book on symbolism and imagery in Horace. What Charles Babcock wrote in a bibliographical survey in 1981 was already true in the 1950s: "Perhaps the most striking change in approach to the lyrics has been an increased appreciation of Horace's use of symbolism and

9. Pasquali 1920, 81–82.

10. A good formulation of the matter by La Penna can be found in his introduction to Pasquali 1966, xxvii.

11. Wilkinson 1945, 129–31.

12. See n. 18 below.

13. Birt 1925 is exceptional.

imagery."[14] The book was Steele Commager's *The Odes of Horace* (1962). The most notable of the articles, one by Niall Rudd, is discussed below.

In the 1960s, a reaction against the New Criticism set in as a new kind of subjective unity was sought. The well-known article on C. 1.9 by Viktor Pöschl will serve as an example for discussion. But the quest for an objective unity was not and has not been abandoned. It persists in the most recent article on this poem.[15] The inertia of this approach, the faith that the unity of the poem lies in the coherence of its references, is perhaps owing to the ideal of historicity. David West, in an attack on symbolism and the notion of subservient imitation of Alcaeus in C. 1.9, stated the historical principle with stark clarity: "Latinists must read with feeling, sometimes with intense feeling, but when they come to propound interpretations or assessments of a poem, they must not be carried away by any feelings which are exclusively modern or inappropriate to the context, but should rather cut out of their minds everything which they can see to be different from what Horace and his original readers would have felt."[16] The mental surgery that West calls for removes all symbolism except that of *virenti canities abest*, which he allows. One of West's arguments against symbolism is that it is favored by American scholars. He cleverly contrives to pardon the Englishman Wilkinson and to condemn Wilkinson's American followers in a single sentence: "Wilkinson's attempt to rescue this poem by symbolical interpretation has won an enthusiastic following, notably in America, but by flattening out the particular references to Horace's personal situation, it reduces the poem to a smooth generalisation, much poorer and less interesting than what Horace actually wrote."[17] In fact, the German Kiessling had

14. Babcock 1981, 1589.

15. Clay 1989.

16. West 1967, 9.

17. West 1967, 11. America is actually a topos. Cf. Culler 1982, 134: "The notion of the 'free play of meaning' has had a fine career, particularly in America, but a more useful concept . . . is. . . ." Culler is engaged in providing the true French version of deconstruction.

seen in C. 1.9 "a thrust into the symbolic" (*einen Stich in das Symbolische*). That was in 1881. Plüss's article of the following year shows that symbolism was an active ingredient in discussion of this ode.[18] A generation earlier, in 1840, Düntzer had claimed to introduce the matter into Horatian studies: "The symbol is very important and in its actual range still hardly recognized in the ancients as a whole and in Horace in particular." He proceeds to define "symbolic" as expression by means of an image (*Bild*), as distinguished from what is expressly said.[19] In C. 1.9, the first stanza provides such an image: "You see how Soracte towers up, white with high snow, how the woods, weighed down, no longer bear their burden, and the rivers are frozen—an image (*Bild*) of age, whose head is grey (cf. *capitis nives*, 4.13.12), which is bent down by the weight of years, and whose youthful life force has grown stiff."[20] In the twentieth century, another German was to discover symbolism,[21] and a Cambridge-educated New Zealander teaching in Canada, Kenneth Quinn, spoke of symbolism three times in his commentary on the ode, undismayed by this association of himself with symbolical interpreters to the south.[22]

But West's anti-Americanism is not at issue here.[23] An exacerbated contradiction in his methodology is of greater interest. With West's historical principle one must compare his practice as a critic. The historical principle is again made clear in the sentence just quoted. Horace spoke directly, in an unmediated voice, as Horace, to his contemporary audience, making references to facts that it is our duty to ascertain. On the basis of these facts, we can see what the

18. Plüss 1882, 55, 60–61.

19. Düntzer 1840, 13. For the symbol in aesthetic theory at the end of the eighteenth century, from which Düntzer's approach clearly derives, see Kermode 1957.

20. Düntzer 1840, 172.

21. Syndikus 1973, 113.

22. Quinn 1980, 140, 142.

23. For West's anti-Americanism cf. West 1973, 53, where again English scholars are pardoned and Americans condemned in the same sentence.

unity of the poem is.[24] But here is the substance of West's final paragraph:

> At the core of this poem he says that when the gods still the winds brawling on the boiling sea, the cypresses stop waving and the old ash trees [do, too]. This general reflection sets off a very complex reaction. It mentions, or suggests to my mind, the violence of the sea, the mythology about the warring winds and the god who pacifies them, the trees which stand out against the Italian horizon, in particular the *ferialis cupressus*, tree of death, but most deeply of all the idea that the gods are concerned with what is vast, violent, and remote, and that by this activity they automatically and without any intention, or any interest, change the view from Thaliarchus' window, and settle his little disturbance. . . . This is one man's Horace and so delicate in the Latin that it protests at being made explicit. It may even not be there at all. But the risk is worth taking to show how rich and suggestive the poetry is.[25]

One notes the use of a metaphor ("at the core") to replace an argument for the centrality of stanza 3 that West's historicist approach could never produce. One is regaled with West's free associations, which are intended, perhaps, to display a sensitivity that he had given us cause to doubt. We are brought near to something "so delicate in *the Latin* that it protests at being made explicit" (my emphasis). These are the words of a reader who has a privileged access to Horace's language. And yet West later disavows accurate knowledge. In the preface to his endnotes, he says that his translations of the odes he discusses "should suggest . . . everything I can see in the Latin *except the level of Horace's language.* B. Axelson's *Unpoetische Wörter* has shown how elusive this is, how much remains to be done on it, and how

---

24. After West invokes Horace's "personal situation" to explain the poem, then Shackleton Bailey (1982, 37 n. 8) invokes the poem, citing West, to show that Horace sometimes visited his Sabine farm during the winter!

25. West 1967, 11–12.

superficial and unsound are most of our labels like 'archaic,' 'collo-
quial,' and so on."[26] The question therefore arises how West, who
insists that Latinists should "cut out of their minds" everything unrelated to the original historical reception of the *Odes*, could, with his
imperfect knowledge of Horace's language, even begin to tackle the
problem of the unity of C. 1.9, let alone respond to the delicacies of
the third stanza.

The contradiction in West between principle and performance
is a curious demonstration of the unfeasibility of the historical demand that West himself articulates. His self-conscious, self-contradic-
tory expression of his personal response to stanza 3 reveals an
engagement with the poem that could never be fully explored and
expressed within the historical-philological parameters West has defined. One senses a reading of the poem lurking behind West's chapter, but this reading can never appear as such. It must take the form
of an attack on other "critics,"[27] with the implicit conventional claim
that the writer is presenting something new. In fact, almost none of
his points are new, and the critics are largely fictitious, as many before
Fraenkel and all after him defended the unity of the poem.

At the opposite pole from West, Niall Rudd (1960) posed the
question: what can study of its imagery contribute to the understanding of the Horace ode? In the case of C. 1.9, he followed in the steps
of M. P. Cunningham (1957) and M. G. Shields (1958), whom he cited
with approval. Rudd found in the images and/or metaphors of the
poem four main pairs of antitheses (winter-spring, age-youth, storm-
calm, anxiety-cheerfulness). He stated:

> Putting the submerged or metaphorical themes in brackets we
> get a scheme [for the sequence of stanzas] like this:
> (1) Winter (age, anxiety).
> (2) Winter, cheerfulness (youth).
> (3) Storm, calm (anxiety, cheerfulness).

26. West 1967, 143 (my emphasis).
27. West 1967, 3 (the first sentence of the chapter): "This poem has been
destroyed by the critics."

(4) Anxiety, cheerfulness, youth.

(5) Age, anxiety, youth, cheerfulness (winter, spring).

(6) Youth, cheerfulness.[28]

Except in a diagram no easier to understand than the list just quoted, Rudd never explains how these antitheses and their metaphorical expression function in the poem to achieve a unity. He presents them as the bare results of an analysis. These results are to be accepted as information *about* the poem, and thus as of the same order as the philological-historical information to which he defers in his introduction, in which he establishes "criteria" that "*ought to govern* the newer mode of analysis" (that is, the analysis of imagery).[29] These criteria, received in the traditional discourse of philology, are of course axiomatic and require no defense. In reading Rudd's article at a distance of thirty years, one cannot help but be more interested in the struggle in his mind between his commitments to two potentially conflicting approaches than in his reading, really the avoidance of a reading, of C. 1.9. As West had to retreat from historicism into a different, more personal kind of criticism, so Rudd has to leave imagery at the stage of analysis and retreat into philology. The attempt to discover a positive objective unity (historical references to Horace's "personal situation") and the attempt to find a positive subjective unity (a pattern of antithetical images) are equally self-defeating.

Pöschl's article of 1966, like West's in the following year, attacks symbolism, "always a danger" and "today it threatens to become a disease." Pöschl begins by establishing an objective unity that is principally a unity of time. The third stanza, he argues, bears no reference to any particular time.[30] It is a piece of folk wisdom. *Et campus et areae* are set off from *lenesque . . . susurri* by *-que*, which introduces a separate, distinct category, so that the soft whisperings have nothing to do with

28. Rudd 1960, 390.

29. Rudd 1960, 373 (my emphasis). The "newer mode of analysis" is already in Düntzer 1840, 172, whose interpretation of the first stanza is the same as Rudd's.

30. Pöschl 1966, 33 (quotations), 35–38.

the Campus Martius and the open spaces of Rome. Everything depends on the interpretation of -*que*.[31] Those places are all for sports, which one can play in the winter, that is, in the time in which the poem is set. So *nunc* (18, 21) refers to the time in which the speaker is speaking. (Thaliarchus could get up and leave the room and follow the speaker's bidding.) The whisperings and also the *angulus* of the last stanza are indoors, so that courtship can go on in the winter, too.

In the course of his demonstration of the objective temporal unity of the poem, Pöschl allows himself a short digression on stanza 3, the same stanza that caused West's thoughts to stray: "I consider it possible that the poet, conceived of as growing old, speaks of the old ash trees with a chuckle, so to say, in order to indicate that he implicates himself in his assertion, that he, too, is beset by storms, whose end he hopes for from the gods. . . . This manner of delicate self-reference, on which I do not wish to insist, but which seems to me to lie within the boundaries of permissible interpretation. . . ."[32] Pöschl feels obliged to apologize for the interpretation he here offers, referring, like Rudd, to axiomatic standards. Indeed, Pöschl has, for a moment, completely changed his method. He explains the ash trees as a reference not to an external fact but as something internal to the poem, something indeed that is only implicit in the poem, namely, the age of the speaker. Pöschl has stumbled into one of the "virtual dimensions" of the poem. As in the case of West's final paragraph, quoted and discussed above, it is stanza 3 that lures the scholar into a departure from his principles (with strikingly different results). This stanza, or the problem of the transition from stanza 2 to stanza 4, is

---

31. For what I believe is the correct interpretation see Dillenburger 1841 on C. 1.21.14; Plüss 1882, 72. Neither is cited by Pöschl (1966), who at 41–42 contents himself with a rejoinder to Pasquali (1920), making it seem that the obvious and customary understanding of -*que* at C. 1.9.19 was Pasquali's brainstorm. Esler (1968–69, 303) has the correct interpretation. She had not seen Pöschl. For a critique of Pöschl's interpretation see Mulroy 1971–72, 77–78. Vretska 1980 merely repeats Pöschl on the matter.

32. Pöschl 1966, 40.

a test of method. I pointed out that West had recourse to a metaphor ("at the core of"). Pöschl ends by referring to stanza 3 as a "hinge" (*Scharnier*) between stanzas 2 and 4.[33] These metaphors and the digressions to which they are related are ways of saying that which cannot be said within the horizon of the scholar's method but which for some reason must be said.

Pöschl's article falls into two halves, of which the first, on objective unity, has now been discussed. The second half begins, "But the particular art of the song lies in its composition. It has a very clear architectonic structure." The subjective unity of the poem will now be demonstrated, and a visual metaphor ("architectonic") immediately presents itself. The poem, Pöschl says, consists of three parts— it is a "triptych." But there are also other principles of form (*Formprinzipien*) that determine the structure of the ode. These principles are again vouchsafed by comparison, now even more explicit, with the visual arts. Pöschl states: "As we know today, contrast is a fundamental element of classical structure." He proceeds to cite an art historian: "Heinrich Wölfflin has shown that in exemplary fashion in his lecture on the 'Beauty of the Classical.'"[34]

But the interrelations of separate parts of a poem cannot be grasped simultaneously for the simple reason that they do not present themselves visually but only in the sequence of reading. The whole matter is in Lessing's *Laokoön*.[35] Pöschl's visual metaphors, like the "hinge" and the digression already discussed, do duty for an argument that it would be very difficult for him to express in other, non-metaphoric terms. The same axiom that governed the demonstration of objective unity governs the demonstration of the subjective unity in terms of "principles of form," those principles that turned out to be visual. Facts about the poem must be established. From these, the interpreter's evidence, a conclusion concerning unity must be drawn.

33. Pöschl 1966, 46.

34. Pöschl 1966, 44, 47–48.

35. Yes, Horace himself said *ut pictura poesis* (*Ars* 361). But he did not say *poesis pictura est*. Also, consider the context of Horace's dictum. Cf. Mitchell 1984.

In the case of objective unity, where the conclusion can be drawn on the basis of a coherent referentiality (for example, everything refers to wintertime), recourse to metaphor is not so necessary. In the matter of subjective unity, if the interpreter is obliged to show a unity in the evidence drawn from the poem, it may be impossible to do so without metaphor.

If metaphor is avoided, then recourse will be had, as in Rudd, to the authority of philology. It was not necessary for Rudd to demonstrate the connections of the images he found in C. 1.9 because the (implicit) rules of his discourse allowed him to present a list of (supposed) facts. A diagram with curving arrows was sufficient demonstration. A similar recourse to authority is found in the final paragraph of a paper from the Ottawa conference (whose first paragraph was quoted at the beginning of this chapter): "The connection of images cannot be mistaken: winter and the frozen trees prepare us for the aged ash trees and the sad cypresses. *Canities* has connections with *candidus*; *virenti* is connected with the trees; winter, the gnome Horace adopted from Alcaeus, has metaphorical links to youth and age. These powerfully connected images guarantee the unity of the poem."[36] What is the source of, or where is, the power that connects the images? The interpreter has not shown that the power is in the poem. Common sense suggests that the connections pointed out by the interpreter are subtle if anything. If they are powerful, if they exert control or force, they must do so in virtue of their nonexplicit effects. In that case, "power" in the passage just quoted might be a metaphor. What of the images' "guaranteeing" the unity of the poem? A guarantee assumes two parties. Here, the images are one party and the poem is the other. For the images to guarantee the poem's unity, they must be separate from the poem. And their separation from the poem, as facts about the poem, is precisely the basis of the paragraph just quoted. The unity of the poem is external to the poem. The power and the guarantee—it does not matter whether or not they

36. Sullivan 1981, 280.

are metaphors—come ultimately from the discourse of philology, which has determined in advance the possible conditions of unity.

At this point my reader may feel that, despite what I said at the beginning of this chapter, I am playing the usual zero-sum game of philology: to the extent that I am right, others must have been wrong, and the way to show how right I am is to cudgel some of the most accomplished Latinists of the twentieth century who have written on C. 1.9. On the contrary, my concern, to repeat, has not been with who is right and who is wrong but with the manner in which representative scholars have dealt with the aesthetic problem of the unity of C. 1.9. I do not regard the Jaussian approach as the only alternative to the philological procedures I have been discussing. (The next chapter faces one of its shortcomings.) The literature on C. 1.9 already contains alternatives, and, as for the more general questions of methodology, the traditions of classical philology already provide different formulations of the two parts of philology with which this chapter began.

As for alternative approaches within the literature on C. 1.9, F. O. Copley's review of Wilkinson in 1946 reported the poet J. V. Cunningham's views on the unity of the poem. Then in 1950, in *The Quest of the Opal: A Commentary on "The Helmsman,"* Cunningham stated:

> as he read on in Horace he came to see that the point of the method lay in the transitions from concrete detail to detail: that the transitions were not elliptical in the sense that the poet had merely omitted a chain of thought which the reader was to supply, and that the details themselves did not imply an abstraction that connected them. The meaning lay in the transitions themselves, in a certain balance of sensibility, a nice adjustment between imagery and statement which met the insoluble problems of life with a controlled use of distraction and irrelevance.

> He analysed the famous Soracte ode (1.9) which begins with an extended description of a midwinter scene and closes with an extended, but in no way parallel, description of a summer love scene. By a relative clause, and in an unemphatic manner,

a description of the equinoctial storms is worked in. The sequence of images gives by implication, but by implication only, the theme: that season follows season, and that time is fleeting. The transitions from image to image are effected by generalised statements that are related to but never state the central theme, so that the point of the poem is qualified by images, whole and concrete in themselves, which cannot be said to illustrate the point. They are not subsumed under it as examples; they are rather digressions that prove to be developments.[37]

This passage never came into the discussion of C. 1.9 in the realm of classical philology, which has its axioms for citation as for proof. These are more complicated than might be expected. It is not only a nonclassicist like Cunningham who does not have to be cited (and thus does not have to be read). There is also an implicit statute of limitations: the article by Plüss (1882) is as worth reading as any other on C. 1.9, but it has been cited only once or twice in the dozens of writings on C. 1.9 in the twentieth century. Certain nationalities are ruled out axiomatically. English and American writers on C. 1.9 rarely cite Italians. At least the first half of Cupaiuolo (1965) seems to me to be as worth reading as any of the dozens of subsequent writers on C. 1.9 who failed to cite him or her.[38]

Though the case of Cunningham prompts reflections on citation that could be carried to much greater length, the real interest of the passage just quoted is its focus on transitions. One could say that the transitions in C. 1.9 are the whole question for the one who wants to show the unity of C. 1.9, precisely the question that is begged when the interpreter pretends that the poem is a visual composition. Pasquali has the merit of facing the question. The visually minded Pöschl rebuked him for "pure fantasy."[39] And yet reflection on Cunningham could have helped those, like Pöschl and Rudd, who wanted to find the unity of the poem in its images. Cunningham adumbrates a way

37. Cunningham 1964, 34–35 = 1970, 176–77.
38. I have only the first initial of the first name.
39. Pöschl 1966, 38. Later, Pasquali is rebuked for "erotic fantasy" (44).

of understanding the relation of the images to the movement of the poem. Pöschl and Rudd can only regroup the images outside of the poem and assert their unity, on the basis of a diagram or a visual metaphor, as the poem's unity.

West, Pöschl, and Rudd all state or imply a philological axiology. They regard their procedure as obligatory. It is the one summed up in the quotation at the beginning of this chapter. But the traditions of classical philology include different formulations of the relation of the two parts of philology that were stated in that quotation. Boeckh's *Encyklopädie und Methodologie der philologischen Wissenschaften* has already made an appearance in this chapter. In conclusion, I return to it for a theoretical account of the two parts of philology. This account reverses the sequence now postulated by classical philology and thus resembles the Jaussian approach. This similarity between Boeckh and Jauss is not surprising, as both derive from the same source, Friedrich Schleiermacher, although Hans-Georg Gadamer and others stand between Schleiermacher and Jauss. Boeckh's great theoretical and methodological opus is divided into two main sections, entitled "Formal Theory of Philological Science" (75–260 = 185 pages) and "Material Disciplines of the Study of Antiquity" (263–853 = 590 pages). The second section contains the "encyclopedia," that is, the survey (with bibliographies) of all the parts of *Altertumslehre*, which have been determined by, and are coordinated by, the concept of philology established in the first part. The formal theory is in two parts: theory of hermeneutics and theory of criticism, in that order. Hermeneutics and criticism are absolute and relative understandings.[40] The goal of hermeneutics "is to understand in its own nature the object itself with which one is concerned," though Boeckh does not deny the need of aids, while "the task of criticism is to understand the relation between two or more objects." The relation of the two is necessarily circular. "The various kinds of exegesis [of individual objects] presuppose real information (*Kentnisse*: plural), and yet this information can be won only through the exegesis of the whole source material." Boeckh sees

40. Boeckh 1886, 55.

the solution of the circle in a mutually reinforcing process, as work on each side, on the individual object and on the constitution of the material disciplines (history of language, grammar, lexicography, and so forth), proceeds.[41] The solution takes place over time, and Boeckh assumes progress. And yet, at any given moment, the interpreter of an individual work will be caught in a circle (as I acknowledged in the opening of chapter 1 above), and perhaps it is for this reason that Boeckh likes to speak of the philological "artist" (Künstler) and of the philological "art" (Kunst) that put into practice the principles of understanding developed within hermeneutics and criticism.[42] At any given moment, the circle must be overcome by art.

Boeckh, however, regards hermeneutics as prior to criticism: "Criticism must everywhere presuppose hermeneutics, the explanation of the individual, in order, from that starting point, to fulfill its own task, to grasp the *relations* of the individual to the embracing whole of its conditions. One can judge nothing without having understood it in itself. Thus criticism presupposes the hermeneutic task as fulfilled."[43] Here, as in many other places, Boeckh also acknowledges the inevitability of circularity. But whether hermeneutics is first or whether hermeneutics and criticism stand in a strictly circular relationship, Boeckh's theory of philology is fundamentally different from the one stated in the quotation at the beginning of this chapter, in which aesthetic understanding is held to be secondary. Indeed, the contradictions in the scholarship on C. 1.9 observed in this chapter can be explained, with reference to Boeckh, as the result of trying to making criticism do the work of hermeneutics. Without attempting an understanding of the work itself, the interpreters discussed in this chapter, using one or another philological method, attempt to ascertain facts about the poem. Pöschl's manner of establishing the meaning of -que, that is, with reference to passages in other

41. Boeckh 1886, 77, 84.
42. Boeckh 1886, 55.
43. Boeckh 1886, 178. His emphasis.

authors, is a case in point.[44] These facts were then secondarily applied to the hermeneutic question of the unity of the poem.

Another of Boeckh's points concerning the chronological relation of hermeneutics and criticism is relevant here: "The beginner must generally practice criticism only in the service of hermeneutics."[45] When it comes to reading a lyric poem, everyone, including the most learned, experienced, and sensitive reader, is a beginner. Everyone must begin by reading the poem. Even the greatest scholar has no other starting point. The manner in which the poem is read, or, as in some cases discussed in this chapter, the manner in which reading is avoided, determines the outcome of criticism and all scholarly activity with respect to the poem. Such an axiom, an alternative to the now prevailing axiology of philology, hardly needs contemporary literary theory; it is already there in Boeckh.

44. In my first reading, with admitted circularity, I relied on the OLD for a standard, very widely attested meaning of -que.

45. Boeckh 1886, 251.

5

. . . .

Fourth
Reading

The preceding chapter showed how the established practice of philology differs from Jaussian reading. Despite their differences, however, the two approaches share some fundamental assumptions. Both are aesthetic and formalistic (the poem is an artistic object that must constitute a unity). Both are historical (the poem can and must be located in a history of literature). Both assume that meaning is deployed in controlled relationships between poet and reader, speaker and addressee (though philology does not always make this latter distinction). In short, both assume an autonomy of the poem, though in the Jaussian approach much of the burden of communication has shifted to the reader.

If, then, between them, the two approaches had said everything possible about C. 1.9, this study of the poem would stop here. And yet a simple thought nags the mind of the Jaussian reader, as it may have been nagging the mind of the reader of this monograph: the central lines of C. 1.9 (quid sit futurum . . .) are commonplaces and Horatian commonplaces in particular. Is it possible to read the poem without somehow accommodating the commonness of these commonplaces? This question becomes all the more urgent when one reflects that another Horatian poem (written earlier, although the historical sequence does not affect the present discussion) possesses remarkable similarities, not only in thought but also in diction and structure, to C. 1.9. This other poem, the Thirteenth Epode, resembles C. 1.9 to a degree that, in all its details, would escape any but a scholarly, critical reading and would, I assume, have escaped, again in all its details, the original audience, too. A comparison of the two poems will lead to a series of parallels in other poems of Horace, and these in turn will form the basis of a deconstructive account of C. 1.9. This account (I avoid the word "reading" on purpose) would, *pro tanto*, overturn the Jaussian readings, and in the concluding chapter the two approaches are balanced against one another.

> Horrida tempestas caelum contraxit, et imbres
>   nivesque deducunt Iovem; nunc mare, nunc silvae
> Threicio Aquilone sonant. rapiamus amici
>   occasionem de die, dumque virent genua
> et decet, obducta solvatur fronte senectus.   5
>   tu vina Torquato move consule pressa meo.
> cetera mitte loqui: deus haec fortasse benigna
>   reducet in sedem vice. nunc et Achaemenio
> perfundi nardo iuvat et fide Cyllenea
>   levare diris pectora sollicitudinibus,   10
> nobilis ut grandi cecinit centaurus alumno:
>   "invicte mortalis dea nate puer Thetide,
> te manet Assaraci tellus, quam frigida parvi
>   findunt Scamandri flumina lubricus et Simois,
> unde tibi reditum certo subtemine Parcae   15
>   rupere, nec mater domum caerula te revehet.
> illic omne malum vino cantuque levato,
>   deformis aegrimoniae dulcibus alloquiis."
>
>   (*Epod.* 13)

A harsh storm has put a frown on the sky, and rain
and snow bring Juppiter down to earth; now the sea, now the
    woods
resound with the Thracian north wind: friends, let's snatch
the opportunity from the day, and while our knees are young
and it's fitting, let's smooth the furrowed brow of age.   5

You broach the wine pressed in the consulship of Torquatus, my
    birth-year.
Don't talk of other things. The god perhaps
will bring these things (our troubles) back to their proper place
    in kindly change. Now with Persian nard
and Mercury's lyre it profits us
to lighten our hearts of dire cares,   10
as the famous centaur sang to his mighty pupil:
"Unvanquished one, mortal son of the goddess Thetis,
the land of Assaracus awaits you that the chill
streams of the little Scamander and the smooth-flowing
    Simois cleave,
your return whence the Fates with thread not
    to be unwoven   15
have broken, and your sea goddess mother will not bring you
    home.
There lighten every care with wine and song,
the sweet consolations of ugly melancholy."

In this poem, as in C. 1.9, a storm is the occasion for exhortation
to drinking (in Epod. 13, song and perfume go along with the drinking). The speaker of the epode addresses friends—the received text
has often been challenged—or a friend.[1] We should drink while we
are still young and can enjoy life. Because the speaker is not here a
senior symposiast, he seeks the warrant for his exhortation in a mythical exemplum, implicitly inferred from the scene in the Iliad (9.186–
89) in which the embassy finds Achilles singing and playing the lyre.
His tutor, the centaur Chiron, had counseled him, according to the
speaker of the epode, to console himself at Troy with wine and song.
And, in the exemplum, Chiron had linked this advice to Achilles'
fated death at Troy. As in the situation to which the exemplum refers,
two hypothetically distinct thoughts are linked: (1) the brevity of life
and (2) wine as an antidote to present cares. These are the two

1. A review of the problem appears in Setaioli 1981, 1737–40.

thoughts that the structure of C. 1.9 holds separate and that became awkwardly joined in Cowper's translation, where the structure of the original was radically changed.

The epode differs from C. 1.9 in the absence of the notion of love as the primary fulfillment of youth. The youth of the epode's addressees is fulfilled in the now of the drinking, which is simultaneous with the situation represented in the poem, whereas the now of Thaliarchus in C. 1.9 proves to belong to the coming season (*nunc et: Epod.* 13.8 ~ *C.* 1.9.18, 21), that is, after the time in which the speaker is speaking. In other respects, however, the epode appears as a reconfiguration of C. 1.9 or vice versa. The "real" storm of the epode affects a totality defined by earth and sea (2–3), like the hypothetical or past storm of the third stanza of C. 1.9. Cares are left to the gods or to the god (*Epod.* 13.7 *deus* ~ *C.* 1.9.9 *divis*). Forget about everything else (*cetera: Epod.* 13.7 ~ *C.* 1.9.9). Youth is "green" (*Epod.* 13.4 *virent* ~ *C.* 1.9.17 *virenti*). To the "real" *puer* Thaliarchus (16) corresponds the *puer* Achilles of the mythical exemplum of the epode (12).

To return to the commonplace of C. 1.9.14–15, the resemblance of this poem to the epode suggests that *quem fors dierum cumque dabit, lucro / adpone* ("set down as gain each day that fortune gives") is another way of saying *rapiamus amici / occasionem de die*, "friends, let's snatch the opportunity from the day" (*Epod.* 13.3–4).[2] The latter does not mean taking some part of the day (cf. *C.* 1.1.20) but, in effect, taking the whole day, for, kept indoors by the storm, they have nothing else to do but to mope if they do not follow the speaker's advice. The day is not to be "set down as gain," as in C. 1.9, but "snatched" or "seized." "The meaning simply is, that the day brings with it this opportunity, and will carry it away out of our reach if we do not promptly lay hands on it."[3] The same thought can be expressed in the metaphor of plucking fruit: *carpe diem* (*C.* 1.11.8). The bookkeeping

2. Shorey and Laing 1927, 500, on *de die*: "i.e. 'which the day presents,' with a further complicating suggestion of *de die bibere, de die convivia facere*, etc." In other words, the speaker exhorts his friends to spend the day drinking.
3. Smith 1896, 379.

metaphor in C. 1.9 now appears somewhat more aggressive. "Set down as gain" does not primarily refer to the act of registering figures in an account book but means something like "capitalize on" or "make profit of."

The essential thought of the commonplace in C. 1.9.14–15 is thus: take what is given. For the notion of the givenness of the present time (*quem fors dierum cumque dabit*), compare *dona praesentis cape laetus horae*, "take the gifts of the present hour and be glad" (C. 3.8.27). A *donum*, "gift" (from *do*, *-are*, "give"), is a thing given. The day is a gift of fortune but it is not like a package left by a delivery man or woman on your doorstep, which is there for you whether you were at home to receive it or not. The gift of time must be actively accepted— snatched, seized, plucked. Such is the Horatian formula for happiness. *Laetus in praesens animus quod ultra est / oderit curare*, "let the mind that is happy in the present disdain to care about the future" (2.16.25–26). It is an ethics of presence, of living in the present. Perhaps the fullest statement of this ethics is found at C. 3.29.41–48:

> ille potens sui
> laetusque deget, cui licet in diem
>   dixisse: vixi. cras vel atra
>   nube polum pater occupato
>
> vel sole puro, non tamen inritum,
> quodcumque retro est, efficiet, neque
>   diffinget infectumque reddet,
>   quod fugiens semel hora vexit.

To paraphrase: That man will live independent and happy who can say, at the end of every day, "I've lived. Tomorrow let the Father occupy the pole of the heavens with a dark cloud or with clear sunshine. He can't make void what's in the past, he can't undo or render undone what the fleeting hour has once brought." Clement Lawrence Smith commented in this way on the distinctions between *inritum*, *diffinget*, and *infectum*: "a deed of gift (for example) may be rendered *void* (*inritum*) before going into effect, by a subsequent deed, superseding it, or it may be modified by *recasting* (*diffinget*), or it may be destroyed and put out of existence (*infectum*); but if the gift has been received *and enjoyed*, then no power can do any of these things."[4] Whether or not a deed of gift lies behind the Latin, this passage from C. 3.29 provides a full expression of the notion of the gift discussed above apropos of C. 3.8.27. Once you take what has been given you, it is always yours. Not even a god can take it back.

As the commonplace of C. 1.9.14 rests on an ethics of presence, it inevitably reminds one of a philosophical commonplace of our own time, the "metaphysics of presence" or the critique thereof by Jacques Derrida. In his view, the whole history of Western metaphysics, up to and including Martin Heidegger, from whom his own project is launched, determines being as presence, no matter what being is called—truth, form, God, the transcendent, and so forth. In Heidegger, being is opposed to forgetfulness and concealment. These contrary aspects of being are themselves part of being at least as its modalities. While being is thus elusive in Heidegger, in Derrida it is nothing but such modalities. This notion is expressed in the Derridean term *différance*. Self-difference (as opposed to the self-identity of being in the metaphysical tradition), postponement, and deferment replace being. Derrida's critique of presence is also stated in terms of "logocentrism." According to Derrida, the history of metaphysics valued spoken speech, the voice, with its immediate, spontaneous signification, over writing. Speech corresponded to presence. But *différance* also applies to speech. Signs refer to other signs and thus are involved in an endless play of signification. A transcendental signified that could control the play of the signifiers disappears in Derrida's critique of presence. Speech therefore already has the attributes traditionally assigned to its inferior counterpart, writing. One of the characteristic findings of Derridean analysis of texts is the breakdown of apparent binary oppositions in this play of the signifiers. These and other apparent structures of the text yield to deconstruction. The text

4. Smith 1896, 259.

is revealed in its textuality as a production necessarily governed by the nature of writing. Writing, in short, is prior to speech, just as *différance* is prior to any semblance of being. Indeed, writing is absolutely prior, and therefore the new science of grammatology must replace philosophy.

The critique of logocentrism as a symptom of the metaphysics of presence proves to have heuristic value for the Horatian ethics of presence. For this ethics entails an ethics of speech. In order to live in the present, one must refrain from speaking about certain things: *cetera mitte loqui*, "don't talk of other things" (*Epod.* 13.7). Wine and song, the main features of the convivium, in which one can live in the present, are themselves expressed in a climactic image of speech: they are the *deformis aegrimoniae dulcibus alloquiis*, "the sweet consolations of ugly melancholy" (*Epod.* 13.18, the last line of the poem). Consolation in this sense is a "speaking to" (*adloquium*, from *ad* + *loquor*, "to speak"). Wine and song are the proper form of "speech," a replacement for speech in the usual sense. Drink, don't talk, because *dum loquimur fugerit invida / aetas*, "while we talk, envious age will have fled" (*C.* 1.11.7–8). In speech, in ordinary talk, we experience the transitoriness of life, we miss the presence of the present.

And yet the present comes to be only through speech. The Horatian speaker uses exhortations and commands to imperceptive or reluctant friends. His own speech creates the present. In the second reading above, some of the speaker's difficulties in representing the present to Thaliarchus came into the open. If, following the lead of Derrida, I scrutinize not the represented or signified time, but the signifiers themselves in their relations to one another, I find another way to describe the speaker's difficulties. The problem discovered in the second reading was the relation of example (*nunc et . . .*) to precept (*quid sit futurum . . .*). The analysis of this precept in relation to other Horatian passages revealed the underlying formula: take what is given. In C. 1.9, the notion of give is expressed by the verb *do, -are* (*dabit*, 14) and the notion of take is expressed in the idiom *lucro / adpone* (14–15), which is synonymous with other statements of the precept in which *rapio, -ere*, and so forth, occur.

The girl's laugh and the bracelet or ring can be placed in the following table of correspondences:

C. 1.9.14–15	dierum . . . dabit	lucro / adpone
C. 1.11.8	diem	carpe
C. 3.8.27	dona . . . horae	cape
Epod. 13.3–4	occasionem de die	rapiamus
C. 1.9.21,23	proditor	dereptum

This rough conjugation of *lucro / adpone* with *dereptum* is encouraged by the collocation of some of these places in a mosaic of Horatian reminiscences found in Seneca:

> crastinum si adiecerit deus, laeti recipiamus [cf. cape laetus 3.8.27]. ille beatissimus est et securus sui possessor qui crastinum sine solicitudine expectat. quisquis dixit "vixi" cotidie [cf. in diem / dixisse: vixi 3.29.42–43] ad lucrum [cf. 1.9.14–15] surgit.
>
> (Sen. Ep. 12.9)

In this light, the examples with which the speaker in C. 1.9 attempts to make the precept enticing take on a new look. The girl's laugh is *proditor* (from *prodo, -ere,* "to give forth" + *tor*), that is, a thing that "gives forth" (C. 1.9.21). Her bracelet or ring is to be *dereptum* (from *de* + *rapio, -ere,* "to seize"), that is, "snatched," "seized" (C. 1.9.23). The examples are thus redundant with the precept: *proditor* repeats *dabit* and *dereptum* repeats *lucro / adpone.*

The language of the example obscurely mirrors the language of the precept. The speaker's description of the tryst is not confirmatory but circular. He does not conclude but repeats himself. The commonplace thus loses its status as a precept confirmed by an example. The commonplace does not control the example any more than the example controls the commonplace. The authority of the speaker is lost in the specular play of the language. The relationship between the speaker and Thaliarchus is not only inverted hierarchically, as the second reading showed, but neutralized, as the hortatory ground of the relationship collapses.

Further, the girl (or girls; cf. the remarks in chapter 2) ceases to be a particular instance of the general precept *nec dulcis amores / sperne* (15–16), which is offered as an antidote to concern about the future and as an exhortation to the fulfillment of youth. From this new perspective, the girl takes on the characteristics of time itself, of the days that offer gifts to be seized. She is no longer an example of what the day gives (14), she gives as the day gives and must be seized like the day's opportunities. Whereas from the point of view of the speaker's rhetorical stance toward Thaliarchus the girl was only an example, in the deconstructed form of the speaker's precept she becomes an actor. As an example, she is submissive, to entice Thaliarchus; as a figure of time, she is active and a force superior to Thaliarchus. As an example, she has her body scanned into parts, arm and finger, and expresses herself in a laugh; as figures of time, these parts, this sound she makes stand in contradiction to the notion of a *pignus* for the future and indicate rather the mortality of Thaliarchus that was the speaker's fairly explicit starting point (*donec virenti canities abest / morosa*, 17–18). His repeated attempts to get the girl or a girl are a "detour to death."[5]

What is to be made of the other relationship, the one between the reader and Horace, which emerged in the first two readings? The intertextuality of C. 1.9 with Alcaeus and other poets seemed to function as a code that expressed, among other things, Horace's *aemulatio*. This code would work successfully only if the reader knew what was copied, what was not, what was imitated, what was not—in short, if the reader knew what was original. And it is Horace's ostensible program to demonstrate his originality (cf. the discussion of the sequence C. 1.1–9 in chapter 3 above). This originality would be the pure Horace in the poetry (cf. the well-known title *Plautinisches im Plautus*). Indeed, a vast scholarly effort has gone into the identification of Greek and Hellenistic echoes of various kinds in Latin poetry, each isolable instance is set down as gain, and types of "influence" are classified. In principle, in any Latin poem, as in C. 1.9, it ought to be

5. Cf. chap. 2, n. 28, above on *repetantur*.

possible to find the poet himself or herself. The poet, if original in some respect, ought to be present in his or her originality.

Despite what T. S. Eliot said about the poet's stealing rather than borrowing, the intertextual elements of a Latin poem do not become its exclusive property; they do not cease to be signifiers in the Greek texts from which they came. Their new existence in Latin does not make them entirely new signifiers and does not confer on them a new, independent signification. By convention, the name Thaliarchus refers to, signifies, a Roman. And yet Thaliarchus is the junior symposiast of archaic Greek poetry. Scholars have argued over his status again and again: is he a slave or is he a freeborn Roman friend of Horace?[6] But whatever he may be, he is in the first instance a crossbreed of Greek and Roman. Even the fact that he receives orders in stanza 2 may be an aspect of his intertextuality. He plays a role like that of Sappho's brother, who was a cupbearer to the nobles in Mytilene (Sappho Test. 203 Voigt). The mythical paradigm is Ganymedes (Il. 20.232–35).[7] It seemed that, for the *aemulatio* of Horace to succeed, Thaliarchus would have to become a Roman, and, if the poem is read, as it was read in chapter 2, with an eye on the relationship between speaker and addressee, and on the possible representation or signification of the presence of the present, this transformation does take place. But if, as already in this chapter, attention is shifted to the signifier, a totally Horatian Thaliarchus never appears, and thus a completely original, strictly non-Alcaic Horace never appears, either. For intertextuality itself, by virtue of which Thaliarchus is a crossbreed, is the code, and, if it is to function as a code, it cannot give up its signifiers and cease to be intertextual. At best, it can qualify and redirect their possible signification. While, from a traditional philological point of view, the Alcaic model for C. 1.9 provides information en-

6. Thaliarchus is a slave: Plüss 1882, 55; Wilamowitz 1913, 311; Birt 1925, 37. Thaliarchus is not a slave: Nohl 1915, 22; Pasquali 1920, 80–81, 85; Smereka 1930–31, 318 n. 22; Catlow 1976, 76–77; Vessey 1985, 31.

7. Hermes also poured wine for the gods: Sappho 141 Voigt = 24 Lobel-Page.

abling the scholar to assess the originality of Horace by an almost mathematical process of reckoning similarities and differences, these are not facts that can be isolated from the two poems but are always in a state of transition from the Greek to the Latin poem. The intertextual code keeps the similarity and the difference in play. For Horace to be a *lyricus vates*, he must remain and be *lyricus*, that is, Greek. For this reason, the scholarly debate about Horace's imitation of Alcaeus can have no end; the debate itself is a symptom of the intertextual play. The originality of Horace will never appear. His *aemulatio* can never be absolutely successful if success is defined as originality. Just as in chapter 2 there proved to be no original performing voice of Horace that could be a sure foundation for the poem's meaning, so there is no absolute artistic originality that can be factored out of the poem's intertextuality.

The intertextual elements of C. 1.9 are also signifiers in relation to the nonintertextual signifiers in the poem and thus involved in yet another play of différance. The rivers are Alcaic; the cypresses and ashes are Roman. The rivers and trees are heterogeneous but belong to the same country. This difference is repeated within the pairing of the two kinds of trees, the native Roman ashes and the Greek or at least Greek-sounding cypresses (*cupressus*; cf. Gr. κυπάρισσος).[8] The landscape is thus not a description that Horace presents to the reader in simple contrast with a Greek original or originals. Some of its elements are intertextual, but these have no significance by themselves. They function with, for example, a trite Latin phrase like *alta . . . nive* to produce a landscape that consists of a play of sameness and difference or of similarity and dissimilarity with other poems, probably not only Greek but also Roman. The wine is native but also Theocritean, and it is served from a jar that is native but has a Greek name. The wine that the Greek-named Thaliarchus will drink is neither Greek nor Roman—and thus not a declaration of Roman indepen-

---

8. Either the Latin word comes from the Greek, or both come from an unknown third language.

dence by Horace—but something between Greek and Roman, like Thaliarchus himself.

If the play of difference and similarity is never decided (because the play of the signifiers never ends in a decision), then the intertextual elements of the poem are not the decipherable code they seemed to be in the first, second, and third readings, and the *aemulatio* of Horace can never win out, no matter how insistent. The relationship of Horace and reader thus suffers the same fate as the relationship of speaker and Thaliarchus. The same collapse of the structure of signification affects both relationships equally. The authority of the author is no greater than the authority of the speaker.

A related point can be made concerning the skeleton at the banquet discussed in chapter 3 as an aspect of the intertextuality of C. 1.9 with a particular Roman sympotic theme. In that discussion, it was concluded that, as in the case of Lucretian Epicureanism, Horace had invoked the recollection of other texts (and works of art) only to repudiate them, in order thus to give a particular contrary cast to his own poem. But if the various indications of the sympotic theme, including the precepts, are regarded not as signifieds but as signifiers, then they continue to maintain a relationship with the larger set of signifiers to which they belong, a relationship of differance. For an aspect of differance is the trace, the reference (for which Derrida and Derrideans use the metaphors of "imprint" and "inscription") by which each signifier is related to the others from which it is absent.

C. 1.9 selects from a group of related themes of the convivium: wine, perfume, garlands, friendship, love, pleasure, the thought of the uncertainty of tomorrow, the exhortation to enjoy life now, and the thought of death. The texts surveyed in chapter 3 show, however, that the thought of death is central. It is the warrant for the other maxims. The skeleton at the banquet enforces the maxim: "get what you can, enjoy it while you may." Death is the chief threat and spur to the enjoyment of life. When, therefore, Horace introduces the sympotic commonplaces of C. 1.9.13–15, even if death is absent, it is the trace that these commonplaces necessarily bear. They do not refer to or allude to or imply death—indeed, the rhetoric of the speaker intends to replace the thought of death with the hope of love, contrary to Propertius at the convivium—but as signifiers they bear death as an inevitable trace.

As a sort of confirmation of this point, it can be observed that several scholars have talked about death in C. 1.9. Although their intuition was good, restricted by the parameters of their methodology, they were forced to connect the idea of death with something stated in the text—usually Soracte or the cypresses—with dire consequences for the reading of the poem as the aesthetic whole they assumed it to be.[9] The skeleton at the banquet could never come and, so far as I know, has never come into discussion of C. 1.9, because there is nothing in the text to which the skeleton can be linked.[10]

9. Segal 1981, a more sophisticated appreciation of the presence of death in C. 1.9, is exceptional.

10. Hommel 1951 is an exception, though Hommel regarded the skeleton at the banquet as only another example of "coarsened Epicureanism" like Horace's: "it is well known how closely the facile sophistication of this poem corresponds to the coarsened Epicureanism of that time" (220).

Conclusion

· · · · · · · · · · · ·

The first three chapters, taking Jauss's essay on Baudelaire's "Spleen" as a model, offered three successive readings of Horace, C. 1.9, as a test of the usefulness of Jauss's method for the reading of an ancient poem. Some revision of this method was necessary even in the first reading in order to meet the historical demands placed on the reader of a poem in an ancient language. Jauss himself, however, had already introduced into his first reading a "commentator with scholarly competence" whose contributions to the reading are indicated by means of indentation.[1] In effect, he divided the first reader into two, one of them aesthetic and the other scholarly. The latter's comments are mostly on syntax, metrics, rhyme, and the like. Such a division would have been almost comical in the reading of an ancient poem, as the scholarly reader would have become a donkey carrying grammars, handbooks, dictionaries, and commentaries. For the aesthetic response to an ancient poem, the historical information from these sources cannot be merely supplemental but must already be in the possession of the reader if any aesthetic response is to occur. For this reason, I combined Jauss's aesthetic and scholarly readers into one.

Though history thus had to be allowed its *et in Arcadia ego*, the first reading remained an Arcadia undisturbed by any direct intervention from the surrounding world of classical scholarship. An adequate reading could be obtained without the interruption and labor

1. Jauss 1982, 144.

of research on particular points, which would in fact have obstructed the first reading. Because the goal of this reading was not to produce new information and thereby to demonstrate scholarly originality, citation of previous work on C. 1.9 was unnecessary. A fortiori, a display of odium toward other scholars was unnecessary. Only four articles were cited, of which three were the only ones I had encountered that presented something like the Jaussian first reading, even though they had originated in other methodologies and the authors' readings were at variance with mine.

In the various imbrications of meter with sense, sense with sound, and so forth, the tone of the speaker of the ode emerged and thus his relationship to the addressee, and this tone proved, in its modulations, to have a structuring effect. One did not have to begin, it seemed, from the supposed two "halves" of the poem (Pöschl's Gedichtehälfte),[2] any more than one had to begin—or could have begun—to read the poem on the basis of an abstract metrical analysis, without a grasp of the metrical sense units. The Alcaic model (338 Lobel-Page) lying behind C. 1.9 involved the reader in another relationship, one between himself and Horace, since Horatian allusions to Alcaeus could not be understood as aspects of the communication of the speaker to the addressee. Within the aesthetic horizon of the first reading, however, this second relationship could not be fully explored, as it would have required the historical context of Horatian aemulatio that could only, given the method, appear in the second and third readings.

The second reading looked to "significance still left open" by the first, to questions posed by the first. Here and there one could rely on the findings of other scholars. In some places, research was necessary, although again scholarly originality was not the goal. The first reading showed that the landscape of the first stanza was to some degree personified as unhappy. How then did Soracte fit in? It was necessary to try to learn more about the mountain. Similarly, the climactic position of diota, along with other things in the immediate con-

---

2. Pöschl 1966, 49. Cf. Cupaiuolo 1965, 283–85; Haffter 1972, 174.

text, drew attention to this *hapax*. What did it convey to Thaliarchus? What did it convey to the reader? Besides these questions, requiring, at least in the first place, historical-philological exploration, a larger question concerning the relationship of the speaker to Thaliarchus remained from the first reading. Could one interpret what seemed to be the emotional intensity behind the commonplaces of lines 13–15 by understanding the concrete advice of lines 15–24 as recollections of the speaker's past as well as projections of Thaliarchus' future? Could this combination of advice and recollection succeed, on the dramatic plane, within the setting of the poem, in overcoming the logical contradiction lurking in the maxim, count each day as gain? The positive answer to these questions then left the question of Horace's relationship to the reader, which had been shaped by Alcaic allusion. It turned out that the development of this other relationship had proceeded pari passu with the one between the speaker and Thaliarchus. For as the younger man was directed away from the sympotic setting provided in the Alcaic model and as the older man in effect renounced the authority conferred upon him by his sympotic role, that is, as the model was abandoned, the reader experienced the successful paraenesis to Thaliarchus as the success of Horace's *aemulatio*.

In the first two readings, more historical matter came in than Baudelaire's "Spleen" had required of the Jaussian model. In the third reading, where history is wanted in order to establish the response of the original audience, Jauss had an advantage in the relative historical closeness of "Spleen" to himself. For a poem by Horace, direct historical evidence was lacking, and it was necessary to follow roundabout paths. The position of C. 1.9 in the careful arrangement of the parade odes afforded a perspective on the varying personae of the poet and thus suggested a question, concerning love, to which this ode would have been read as (at least) a partial answer, whereas in the first and second readings offered here, love was only incidental to the question of time or of the passage of time in an individual life. The original audience also had expectations of the poem based on the literary tradition of the text. From this angle of historical vision, too, love loomed larger. For it seemed that pederasty would have been assumed for Alcaeus and for the particular Alcaic model of C. 1.9, and therefore the erotic advice given Thaliarchus in stanzas 3 to 6 would have appeared as the complete abdication of the expected role of the senior symposiast.

Jauss also called for ascertainment if possible of the history of reception, of responses to the poem intervening between the original audience's and the present reader's. The scholiastic titles provided material for comparison with the modern, romantic title "The Soracte Ode." In addition to these stages of reception, that is, the original one, the late antique and medieval (scholiastic), and the romantic, it was possible to catch glimpses of others beginning in the seventeenth century and overtaking the romantic in the nineteenth. Translations of C. 1.9 showed how this ode had been read at various points in this long modern period. Convergences between the translations and scholarship on C. 1.9 appeared. Cowper, sometimes considered a precursor of the romantics, found it impossible to bring the speaker's erotic advice into his translation. The problem of the two "halves" was already at hand. Cowper, who could read only half of the poem, anticipates Byron, who could read none of it, though Byron believed that, because of its assumed feeling for Soracte, the poem would have caused him raptures if his Latin had put it within his reach. C. 1.9 became unreadable, then (Goethe was another case), just at the time that nineteenth-century classical philology was defining its new scientific project. (For example, Boeckh began in 1809 to give the lectures on which his *Encyklopädie und Methodologie der philologischen Wissenschaften* was based.) A clear symptom of the unreadability of C. 1.9 is the translation by the classicist Conington. But C. 1.9 was to return to favor as "The Soracte Ode," that is, in a romanticized form. Though great romantics like Byron and Goethe had no use for the Horatian ode, they invented a new sensibility within which a new appreciation of C. 1.9 became possible, as in Fraenkel's grudging remarks concerning his vision of Soracte from Rome.

In the present study of C. 1.9, reading self-consciously returns, though from hermeneutics not from classical philology. A conflict between hermeneutics and philology, already indicated in chapter 1 apropos of metrics and versification, became the theme of chapter 4. Though the two approaches were comparable with respect to their shared goal of discovering the aesthetic unity of the poem, reading became a criterion by which hermeneutics could be distinguished from philology. Whereas for hermeneutics the poem is a processive structuration appearing within the horizon of reading or readings, for philology the poem must be a restructuration on the basis of evidence gleaned from analysis. The restructuration takes place according to axiomatic rules of evidence that are coordinated with apparently congenial approaches—biographical-historical (West), New Critical (Rudd), logical-formalistic (Pöschl). In each case, rather glaring self-contradictions showed that the scholar's purported empiricism was spurious. The unity that he discovered was less in the poem than in the discourse belonging to his method. For that reason, the scholar typically referred to his procedure in deontic terms, strengthening his own discourse as the prop of the poem's unity.

The fourth chapter ended by invoking the traditions of classical philology, in the form of the authority of August Boeckh, for a new formulation of the relation of hermeneutics and reading, on the one hand, and philology in its critical function ("to understand the relation between two or more objects"), on the other, and for the stipulation of the priority of the former. Willy-nilly, I adopted the deontic mode of the scholars mentioned in the preceding paragraph, though not to repudiate some other approach in the name of philology but to suggest a rapprochement of philology and hermeneutics. The discussion of C. 1.9 might thus have come to an end with the fourth chapter, now that hermeneutics and philology had both had their say. But history repeated its refrain. The reader knew of another, specifically Horatian dimension of the poem that had not been explored in the third, historicist reading. Why was this Horatian dimension absent from the third reading? The answer lies in the principle of reading. The Lucretian-Epicurean resonances of C. 1.9 and the poem's intertextuality with a particular Roman sympotic theme could be assumed to belong to the experience of the original readers of the poem. Though the specifically Horatian dimension of C. 1.9 is certainly available to any reader, ancient or modern, the details of the *carpe diem* theme that formed the basis of the deconstruction of the poem could appear only in a philological and linguistic analysis that was motivated by the Jaussian readings in the sense that it responded to something left over by them, unaccommodated by them but which could not be integrated into them. The relation of C. 1.9.13–15 to other Horatian commonplaces was not a matter of intertextuality: C. 1.9.13–15 were not allusions to other places in Horace.

The analysis of the commonplaces thus did two things that would hardly form part of the normal experience of the reading of a single poem. First, it scrutinized various statements of the *carpe diem* theme to see what might lie behind its apparent banality and triviality. The analysis thus parted company with the aesthetic and interpretative responses of a reader, as distinguished from a scholar focused on particular goals, and even with what is likely to be the usual scholarly sense of the philosophic commonplaces in Horace. Consider the view of Paul Shorey:

> the criticism of life is a blending of Stoic didacticism with gently Epicurean melancholy in the urbane tone of a man of the world, member of a metropolitan and imperial society. That life is short, that the bloom of the rose is brief, that the bird of time is on the wing, that death comes to prince and pauper alike, that it is pleasant to be young and in love but that you "know the worth of a lass once you have come to forty year," . . .—such are the eternal commonplaces that Horace is ever murmuring in our ears.[3]

Under scrutiny, however, certain of these commonplaces proved to have not only the similarity of content that Shorey emphasizes but also an interesting similarity of diction. Second, prompted by a reminiscence of Derrida, the analysis willfully and experimentally applied the observations on diction to C. 1.9, treating the maxims of that poem not as ideas signified but as signifiers. The great remoteness of

3. Shorey and Laing 1927, xvii–xviii.

this procedure from reading can be seen in the fact that the analysis of C. 1.9.21–23 (*proditor; dereptum*) required the deployment of these terms in a kind of conjugational set of relations with synonymous terms. One can compare Paul de Man's critique of Jauss's reading of "Spleen," which begins by translating, as it were, a passage of "Spleen" into Hegelian terms in order then to reverse Jauss's interpretation of this passage.[4]

My analysis, then, was undertaken as apart from a reading of the poem as a whole and therefore belonged to what Boeckh called "criticism," to that fundamental impulse of philology "to understand the relation between two or more objects." In this respect, that is, in their analytic starting points, and in their dependence on relational aspects of the object to be analyzed, philology and deconstruction are, paradoxically, the same. Deconstruction is liable to the same charge as philology: just as philology displaces the unity of the poem into its own discourse, so deconstruction dissolves that unity with reference to particular points in the poem that have been chosen on the basis of prior assumptions. Jaussian hermeneutics, for its part, thematizes such assumptions in the concept of the horizon of expectation.

I have referred to the beginning of the deconstructive move in the last chapter as inspired by a reminiscence of Derrida. As such, this move was hardly necessary; and, in fact, as opposed in principle to the Jaussian readings, it could hardly be expected to add anything to them. The question of motive, by which I mean intellectual or scholarly, not psychological motive, remains to be answered. This is a question that de Man felt obliged to face when he made the deconstructive turn against Jauss's reading of "Spleen" to which I have referred above. This turn, prepared by a series of reflections on Jauss's neglect of the play of the signifier, comes at the point at which de Man says: "The assurance that further questioning [of Jauss's interpretation] . . . should take place has little to do with one's own spleen, with pessimism, nihilism or the historical necessity to overcome

4. Jauss 1982, xxv (de Man's introduction) = de Man 1985, 71–72.

alienation. It depends on powers of poetic analysis, which it is in no one's power to evade."[5] What is of interest here is not so much the denial of personal responsibility but the invocation, as against well-known forms of historical determinism, of a new kind of determinism called "poetic analysis," which is, in the context, obviously nothing but a particular Derridean doctrine now presented as having a life and necessity of its own. In practice, however, as de Man's own performance shows, this analysis cannot take place except as against a text that has already been read and interpreted or a text that is presumed to have been read and interpreted in a certain way. For that matter, there must be something in the first place that presents itself as a text, that makes implicit claims to be a text.

My own motive was the hope that I could find the points in the poem that would allow me to deconstruct it and thus to institute a comparison between the methods and the results of two approaches that I already (not always but already) knew represented the fundamental alternatives for the reading of a lyric poem (and perhaps for all kinds of literature). At this point in my conclusion, Jauss and Derrida or deconstruction become nothing but rubrics for these alternatives, each of which has various exponents and is supported by various bodies of theory and by now has a considerable history.[6] On the side of deconstruction, the text is a fragile surface that must be penetrated and revealed in terms of its production. The instrument is critical (in the Boeckhian sense) philology enhanced by linguistics. On the other side, the text is an aesthetic object, promising pleasure, intellectual interest, and communication. The instrument is hermeneutics. Intertextuality is a good index of the difference between these approaches. For deconstruction, intertextuality is only an aspect of the textuality of the text, of the conditions prior to and "inscribed" in the text, conditions that ultimately the text cannot master. For the rival approach, intertextuality is a fundamental means of con-

---

5. Jauss 1982, xxiv (de Man's introduction) = de Man 1985, 71.

6. For Jauss's development from the 1960s up to *Toward an Aesthetic of Reception* see Irmgard 1984.

stituting the poetic text. For example, in a series of valuable studies Gian Biagio Conte has shown how poetic allusion has the same function as the rhetorical trope, how poetic allusion serves to articulate and define the individual text within its tradition.[7]

Though my own preference is for "Jauss" and for Jauss, I believe that deconstruction has a contribution to make. The gain that came from my deconstructive nonreading of C. 1.9 was the girl, who had remained as passive in my readings of the poem as she was in the speaker's presentation of her to Thaliarchus. The perspective of my first and thus of my second reading was the relationship between the speaker and Thaliarchus, which, from the Alcaic model and from other features of the poem, I inferred to be that of an older to a younger man. From this perspective, the girl could never appear as anything but an aspect of the speaker's rhetoric. When, however, the Horatian commonplaces of C. 1.9.13–15 were regarded not as things signified to Thaliarchus but as signifiers, the description of the girl and Thaliarchus' encounter with her acquired new implications. The

---

7. Conte 1986. I have placed Conte on the side of "Jauss," where it is certain that he belongs. It should be pointed out, however, that Conte criticizes the notion of "horizon of expectation" and prefers the notion of the "Model Reader," a reader prefigured in the text (30 n. 13). I would suggest that intertextuality as demonstrated by Conte could never have become known to anyone but a scholar unless readers had in fact already read the texts that the poet uses to create the Model Reader. These texts have already shaped the horizon of expectation of empirical, historical readers. I observe, further, that despite the explicit tension between traditional philology and Conte's thesis on intertextuality (which is refreshing and valuable), Conte's preference is for a text that remains an object of study concerning which the philologist produces positive findings. But the reader that Conte would like to keep inside the text is always in danger of escaping. Consider this sequence of sentences: "When considered from within the text, i.e., from the standpoint of the text in relation to the reader who is prefigured in the text, typology can be defined as convention. For the reader a series of narrative constants organizes the text according to a system of expectations" (30 n. 12). Is not the reader in the second sentence an empirical reader outside the text?

conquest would ultimately be the girl's, not Thaliarchus', for she was only another figure of time.

This finding can now be brought into relation with a "significance still left open" even after the various readings of the poem and the consideration of other approaches in chapters 4 and 5. The modern reader may see the final stanza of the poem within the horizon of his or her own observations of Italy or of reports of women who have traveled in Italy or of both. Within this horizon Thaliarchus is a prototype of the "Latin lover," the incredibly persistent (*repetantur* [20] is an understatement) Italian suitor or woman chaser. The speaker's program for Thaliarchus seems to contain the erotic destiny of his race. The woman's role in this destiny, token resistance, is unquestioned within the perspective of the speaker, Thaliarchus, and their descendants. The deconstructive perspective, however, offers a kind of conquest or triumph on the part of the girl, who is liberated from her status in the speaker's rhetoric and thus from her assumed role. This result of deconstruction could be accommodated to a new reading of C. 1.9, occurring within a new horizon of expectation, just as, at the end of chapter 4, it was proposed that philological criticism be accommodated to hermeneutics.

My own horizon of expectation was, it seems, based in my own gender, and it would have been for that reason that the particular significance discussed in the preceding paragraph was, and is, still left open. In accordance with the Jaussian method, however, my own horizon ought to be definable on the basis of the third reading, that is, in comparison with the original readers' horizon, and to that comparison I now turn. I find two main areas of difference. First, time presented itself to me as the main problem, and, as one accustomed to complex, intellectually challenging twentieth-century poetry, I concentrated on the subtle difficulties of the speaker's representation of time to Thaliarchus. Despite, or because of, this focus of my attention, I followed the speaker in avoiding a direct confrontation with the implicit idea of death. Only in the third reading, in the dimension of intertextuality, did the skeleton at the banquet appear; he would, I believe, have been more present in the minds of Horace's contemporary readers, who would have been more sensitive to the poet's reshaping of sympotic themes. Second, both the contextualization of C. 1.9 in the sequence of the parade odes and the intertextuality of C. 1.9 with Lucretius suggested an ethical concern that was not detected in my first and second readings. As the intertextuality of *dulcis* (15) with Roman love poetry shows,[8] Horace is staking out for Thaliarchus and his ilk a particular licit area of romantic-sexual activity, as Cicero had already done for young men in *pro Caelio* (42). To the twentieth-century bourgeois reader, neither this activity in particular nor sexuality in general presents itself as a pressing ethical question, and therefore the text does not present itself as an answer to such a question. For Horace and his readers, however, the question was, I believe, open. Their Hellenized state of mind is the one described by Michel Foucault in *The Use of Pleasure* and in part 1 of *The Care of the Self*: they are guided not by a moral code based on sexual acts and sexual objects but by the style of the use of these acts and objects for sexual pleasure.[9] The ethical question is what this style should be, and C. 1.9 provides an answer that applies to a particular age group, balancing the use of sexual pleasure against other activities appropriate to this time of life (*et campus et areae*, 18) but suggesting the primacy of the former.

With the comparison of the horizons of expectations, the present reader's and the original readers', the Jaussian task is completed. Because the present reader was a classicist and because the present state of literary theory was what it is, the task could never have remained innocent of possibly hostile surroundings. Indeed, from the side of hermeneutics, philology and deconstruction took on an eerie similarity. Hermeneutics, however, proved to be a friendly neighbor, offering cooperation, not scorn and denial, in the project of reading, and even offering its house as a place of refuge in case of need.

8. Cf. Vessey 1985, 36.

9. Foucault 1985 and 1988. Cf., again, Shackleton Bailey 1982, 41–42, for what may have been Horace's own experience in this area. When I speak of Horace's readers, I refer not to the average freeborn Roman but to the sexually mobile echelon to which Horace belonged.

Bibliography

. . . .

The list of editions and commentaries includes only those that I used. It is not intended to be exhaustive. This list is followed by a general bibliography and by a chronological list of works on Odes 1.9. The latter is a subset of the former, with occasional comments, and serves as a timeline for chapter 4.

Editions and Commentaries: Horace

Acro. *See* Pseudo-Acro.

Bentley, Richard. 1869. *Quintus Horatius Flaccus.* 3d ed. Berlin: Weidmann.

Borzsák, S., ed. 1984. *Quinti Horatii opera.* Leipzig: Teubner.

Döring, Friedrich G. 1831. *Q. Horatii Flacci opera.* Oxford: D. A. Talboys.

Duentzer, Heinrich. 1859. *Q. Horatii Flacci opera.* Braunschweig, London, and Paris: G. C. E. Meyer.

Fea, Charlès. 1827. *Q. Horatii Flacci opera.* Vol. 1, ed. F. H. Bothe. Heidelberg: A. Osswald.

Grävius, Joannes G. 1827. *Scholia ad Horatii odarum libros duo priores.* Mannheim: Kathol. Bürgerhospitals-Buchdruckerey. Separately paginated (1–69) and bound with Fea 1827 at the end of the volume.

Hauthal, Ferdinand. 1966. *Acronis et Porphyrionis commentarii in Q. Horatium Flaccum.* Amsterdam: P. Schippers. Reprint of the 1864 edition, Berlin: Julius Springer.

Holder, Alfred, ed. 1894. *Pomponi Porfyrionis commentum in Horatium Flaccum.* Innsbruck: Wagner.

Keller, O., ed. 1967. *Scholia in Horatium vetustiora.* Vol. 1. Stuttgart: Teubner. Reprint of the 1902 edition.

Kiessling, Adolf, and Richard Heinze. 1917. *Q. Horatius Flaccus: Oden und Epoden.* 6th ed. Berlin: Weidmann. Eleventh edition (1964) has bibliography by Burck.

Klingner, F., ed. 1970. *Quinti Horatii opera.* Leipzig: Teubner.

Lambinus, Dionysius. 1596. *In Quintum Horatium Flaccum.* 4th ed. Frankfurt.

Nisbet, R. G. M., and Margaret Hubbard. 1970. *A Commentary on Horace: Odes Book I.* Oxford: Oxford University Press.

Numberger, Karl. 1972. *Horaz: Lehrer-Kommentar zu den lyrischen Gedichten.* Münster: Aschendorf.

Orelli, J. G. 1886. *Q. Horatius Flaccus.* 4th ed. Revised by J. G. Baiter and W. Hirschfelder. 2 vols. Berlin: S. Calvary.

Porphyrio. *See* Holder.

Pseudo-Acro and Porphyrio. *See* Hauthal; Holder; Keller.

Quinn, Kenneth. 1980. *Horace: The Odes.* New York: St. Martin's Press.

Shorey, Paul, and G. J. Laing. 1927. *Horace: Odes and Epodes.* Chicago: Benjamin H. Sanborn.

Smith, C. L. 1896. *The Odes and Epodes of Horace.* Boston: Ginn.

Syndikus, H. P. 1973. *Die Lyrik des Horaz: Eine Interpretation der Oden.* Vol. 1. Darmstadt: Wissenschaftliche Buchgesellschaft.

Tescari, Onorato. 1936. *Quinto Orazio Flacco: I carmi e gli epodi.* Turin: Società Editrice Internazionale.

General Bibliography

Arnold, Theodor. 1891. *Die griechischen Studien des Horaz.* 2d ed. by Wilhelm Fries. Halle a. S.: Verlag der Buchhandlung des Waisenhauses.

Avery, W. T. 1964. "Homeric Hospitality in Alcaeus and Horace." *CP* 59:107–9.

Axelson, Bertil. 1945. *Unpoetische Wörter: Ein Beitrag zur Kenntnis der lateinischen Dichtersprache.* Lund: C. W. K. Gleerup.

Babcock, Charles L. 1981. "Critical Approaches to the Odes of Horace." *ANRW* 2.31.3:1560–1611.

Bagnani, G. 1954. "No Fire without Smoke!," *Phoenix* 8:23–27.

Bailey, Cyril, ed. 1966. *Titi Lucreti Cari De rerum natura libri sex.* Vol. 3. Oxford: Clarendon Press.

Baneke, F. X. J. 1963–64. "De klanken van de Soracte." *Hermeneus* 35:262–65.

Baudelaire, Charles. 1961. *Les fleurs du mal*. Ed. Antoine Adam. Paris: Editions Garnier Frères.

Birt, Theodor. 1925. *Horaz' Lieder und römisches Leben*. Leipzig: Quelle and Meyer.

Blaiklock, E. M. 1959. "The Dying Storm: A Study in the Imagery of Horace." *G&R*, n.s. 6:205–10.

Boeckh, August. 1886. *Encyklopädie und Methodologie der philologischen Wissenschaften*. Ed. Ernst Bratuscheck. 2d ed. by Rudolf Klussmann. Leipzig: Teubner.

Bolgar, R. R. 1964. *The Classical Heritage and Its Beneficiaries: From the Carolingian Age to the End of the Renaissance*. New York: Harper and Row.

Bonnvia-Hunt, Noel A. 1954. *Horace the Minstrel: A Study of His Sapphic and Aeolic Lyrics*. London: Musical Opinion. Reprinted. Kineton: The Roundwood Press, 1969.

Bottkol, J. McG. 1943. "Dryden's Latin Scholarship." *Modern Philology* 40:241–55. Reprinted in *Essential Articles for the Study of John Dryden*, ed. H. T. Swedenberg, 397–424. Hamden, Conn.: Archon Books, 1966.

Bundy, Elroy. 1986. *Studia Pindarica*. Berkeley and Los Angeles: University of California Press.

Burger, C. P. 1926. *Aere Perennius: Scherts en Ernst in de Oden van Horatius*. The Hague: M. Nijhoff.

Byron, George Gordon, Lord. 1922. *The Works of Lord Byron*. Vol. 2, ed. E. H. Coleridge. London: John Murray.

Campbell, Archibald Y. 1924. *Horace: A New Interpretation*. London: Methuen.

Catlow, Laurence. 1976. "Fact, Imagination and Memory in Horace, Odes 1.9." *G&R* 23:74–81.

Christ, W. von. 1868. "Über die Verskunst des Horaz im Licht der alten Überlieferung." *Sitzungsberichte der königlichen bayerischen Akademie der Wissenschaften zu München*, Philos.-philol. Classe 1:1–44.

Clay, Jenny Strauss. 1989. "Horace Ode 1.9: Horace's September Song." *CW* 83:102–5.

Collinge, N. E. 1961. *The Structure of Horace's Odes*. London: Oxford University Press.

Commager, Steele. 1962. *The Odes of Horace*. New Haven and London: Yale University Press.

Conington, John, trans. 1863. *The Odes and Carmen Saeculare of Horace*. London: Bell and Daldy.

Connor, Peter. 1972. "Soracte Encore." *Ramus* 1:102–12.

Conte, Gian Biagio. 1986. *The Rhetoric of Imitation: Genre and Poetic Memory in Virgil and Other Latin Poets*. Ithaca: Cornell University Press.

Cook, Deborah. 1986. "Translation as Reading." *British Journal of Aesthetics* 26:143–49.

Copley, F. O. 1946. Review of Wilkinson 1945. *AJP* 67:280–83.

Costa, C. D. N., ed. 1973. *Horace*. London and Boston: Routledge and Keagan Paul.

Cowper, William. 1926. *The Poetical Works of William Cowper*. Ed. H. S. Milford. London: Oxford University Press.

Culler, Jonathan. 1982. *On Deconstruction*. Ithaca: Cornell University Press.

Cunningham, J. V. 1964. *The Journal of John Cardan. Together with "The Quest of the Opal" and "The Problem of Form."* Denver: Alan Swallow.

———. 1970. "Odes I,9 and a Note from the Quest of the Opal." *Arion* 9:175–77. Cunningham's translation of C. 1.9 and reprint of a passage from Cunningham 1964.

Cunningham, M. P. 1957. "Enarratio of Horace Odes 1.9." *CP* 52:98–102.

Cupaiuolo, F. 1965. "L'Ode I,9 di Orazio." *RSC* 13:278–86.

Delaunois, Marcel. 1962. "Paradoxes et subtilités d'Horace dans les odes du livre premier." *Les études classiques* 30:167–79 and 268–82.

de Man, Paul. 1985. "Lyrical Voice in Contemporary Theory." In *Lyric Poetry: Beyond New Criticism*, ed. Chaviva Hošek and Patricia Parker, 55–72. Ithaca and London: Cornell University Press.

Dillenburger, W. 1841. *Quaestionum Horatianarum Particula I. et II*. Bonn: Habicht.

Dryden, John. 1909. *The Poetical Works of John Dryden*, ed. George R. Noyes. Boston and New York: Houghton Mifflin.

Dunbabin, Katherine M. D. 1986. "Sic Erimus Cuncti . . . The Skeleton in Graeco-Roman Art." *JDAI* 101:185–255.

Düntzer, H. 1840. *Kritik und Erklärung der horazischen Gedichte*. Part 1 (Die Oden). Braunschweig: G. C. E. Meyer.

———. 1843. *Kritik und Erklärung der horazischen Gedichte*. Part 3 (Die Episteln). Braunschweig: G. C. E. Meyer.

———. 1846. *Kritik und Erklärung der horazischen Gedichte*. Part 5 (Nachträge und Berichtigungen). Braunschweig: G. C. E. Meyer.

Edmunds, Lowell. 1988. "Foucault and Theognis." *Classical and Modern Literature* 8:79–91.

Esler, C. C. 1968–69. "Horace's Soracte Ode: Imagery and Perspective." *CW* 62:300–305.

Fairclough, H. R. 1935. *Some Aspects of Horace*. San Francisco: Privately printed.

Fitzgerald, W. H. 1985. "Firewalking on Soracte: A Vergilian Note on Horace Carmen I.9." *Vergilius* 31:59–60.

Foucault, Michel. 1985. *The Use of Pleasure: The History of Sexuality*. Vol. 2, trans. Robert Hurley. New York: Pantheon Books.

———. 1988. *The Care of the Self: The History of Sexuality*. Vol. 3, trans. Robert Hurley. New York: Vintage Books. Hardcover: Pantheon Books, 1986.

Fraenkel, Eduard. 1957. *Horace*. Oxford: Oxford University Press.

Frank, Tenney. 1927. "How Horace Employed Alcaeus." *CP* 22:291–95.

Friedlaender, Ludwig. 1922. *Darstellungen aus der Sittengeschichte Roms*. Vol. 1. 10th ed. by Georg Wissowa. Leipzig: S. Hirzel.

Gagliardi, Donato. 1987. "La barriera sottile del presente: Struttura e senso dell'ode oraziana I.9." *CCC* 8:199–208.

Galiani, Ferdinando. 1910. *Gli studi sopra Orazio dell'abate Ferdinando Galiani*. Ed. Fausto Nicolini. Naples: Francesco Giannini e Figli.

Gelsomino, R. 1962. "Leggendo l'ode del Soracte (Horat. Carm. I,9)." *Helikon* 2:553–71.

Genette, G. 1988. "Structure and Functions of the Title in Literature." *Critical Inquiry*: 14:692–720.

Gentili, B., and G. Perrotta. 1965. *Polinnia: Poesia greca arcaica*. 2d ed. Messina and Florence: G. d'Anna.

Goad, Caroline. 1916. *Horace in the English Literature of the Eighteenth Century*. Yale Studies in English, no. 58. New Haven: Yale University Press.

Gow, A. S. F., ed. 1952. *Theocritus*. Cambridge: Cambridge University Press.

Greenough, J. B., G. L. Kittredge, et al. 1931. *Allen and Greenough's New Latin Grammar for Schools and Colleges*. Boston: Ginn.

Haffter, H. 1972. "Die Soracte-Ode des Horaz (I,9)." *MH* 29:172–76.

Hawthorne, Nathaniel. 1980. *The French and Italian Notebooks*, ed. Thomas Woodson. The Centenary Edition of the Works of Nathaniel Hawthorne, vol. 14. Columbus: Ohio University Press.

Henderson, W. J. 1967. "Horace, *Carm*. I.9: An Analysis." *Acta Classica* 10:11–18.

Highet, Gilbert. 1957. *Poets in a Landscape*. New York: Knopf.

Hofmann, J. B. 1965. *Lateinische Syntax und Stilistik*. Vol. 2. Rev. by Anton Szantyr. Munich: C. H. Beck.

Holub, Robert C. 1984. *Reception Theory: A Critical Introduction*. London and New York: Methuen.

Hommel, Hildebrecht. 1950. *Horaz: Der Mensch und das Werk.* Heidelberg: F. H. Kerle.

———. 1951. "Cetera Mitte: Zu Archilochos, Horaz, Euripides und Empedokles." *Gymnasium* 58:218–27.

Hyde, W. W. 1915. "The Ancient Appreciation of Mountain Scenery." *CJ* 11:70–84.

Irmgard, Wagner. 1984. "Hans Robert Jauss and Classicity." *MLN* 99:1173–84.

Iser, Wolfgang. 1980. "The Reading Process." In *Reader-Response Criticism: From Formalism to Post-Structuralism,* ed. Jane Tompkins, 50–69. Baltimore: Johns Hopkins University Press. Reprinted from Iser, *The Implied Reader: Patterns in Communication in Prose Fiction from Bunyon to Beckett,* 274–94. Baltimore: Johns Hopkins University Press, 1974.

Jauss, Hans Robert. 1982. *Toward an Aesthetic of Reception.* Trans. Timothy Bahti. Theory and History of Literature, vol. 2. Minneapolis: University of Minnesota Press.

Kant, Immanuel. 1929. *Critique of Pure Reason.* Trans. N. Kemp Smith. London: Macmillan.

Keil, Heinrich, ed. 1874. *Grammatici Latini.* Vol. 6. Leipzig. Reprinted. Darmstadt: Olms, 1961.

Kenney, E. J. 1970. "That Incomparable Poem the 'Ille Ego'?" *CR NS* 20:290.

———. 1982. "Books and Readers in the Roman World." In *The Cambridge History of Classical Literature,* vol. 2, ed. Kenney, 3–32. Cambridge: Cambridge University Press.

Kermode, Frank. 1957. *The Romantic Image.* New York: Macmillan.

Keseling, Paul. 1943. "Homerica." *Philologische Wochenschrift* 63:141–42.

Kiessling, Adolf. 1881. "Horatius." *Philologische Untersuchungen* 2:48–122.

Klinz, A. 1967. "Horaz, Carm. I,9—Catull, Carm. 5: Deutung und Vergleich." *Der altsprachliche Unterricht* 10.1:34–41.

Kresic, Stephanus, ed. 1981. *Contemporary Literary Hermeneutics and Interpretation of Classical Texts.* Ottawa: Ottawa University Press.

La Penna, Antonio. 1963. *Orazio e l'ideologia del principato.* Turin: Einaudi.

Lathrop, H. B. 1933. *Translations from the Classics into English from Caxton to Chapman.* University of Wisconsin Studies in Language and Literature, no. 35. Madison: University of Wisconsin Press.

Lebek, W. D. 1981. "Horaz und die Philosophie: Die 'Oden.'" *ANRW* 2.31.3:2031–92.

Lee, M. Owen. 1969. *Word, Sound, and Image in the Odes of Horace.* Ann Arbor: University of Michigan Press.

Lerner, Laurence. 1983. "Titles and Timelessness." In *Reconstructing Literature*, ed. Lerner, 179–204. Totowa, N.J.: Barnes and Noble.

Levenston, E. A. 1978. "The Significance of the Title in Lyric Poetry." *Hebrew University Studies in Literature* 6.1:63–78.

Lobel, Edgar, and Denys Page, eds. 1963. *Poetarum lesbiorum fragmenta*. Oxford: Clarendon Press.

Lockyer, Jr., C. W. 1968. "Horace Odes I,9." *CJ* 63:304–8.

McDermott, E. A. 1977. "Greek and Roman Elements in Horace's Lyric." *ANRW* 2.31.3:2031–92.

———. 1981. "Horatius Callidus." *AJP* 98:363–80.

MacKay, L. A. 1977. "Horatiana: Odes 1.9 and 1.28." *CP* 72:316–18.

Manitius, M. 1893. *Analekten zur Geschichte des Horaz im Mittelalter (bis 1300)*. Göttingen: Dieterich'sche Verlagsbuchhandlung.

Merrill, E. T. 1901. "Horace, Carm I.9.1 and I.2.14." *CR* 15:128–29.

Minadeo, Richard. 1982. *The Golden Plectrum*. Amsterdam: Rodopi.

Mitchell, W. J. T. 1984. "What Is an Image?," *New Literary History* 15.3:503–37.

Molina, M. 1955. "Horacio, Carm. I,9 Vides ut alta . . ., versión y comentario." *Palaestra Latina* 149:27–32.

Moritz, L. A. 1976. "Snow and Spring: Horace's Soracte Ode Once Again." *G&R* 23:169–76.

Moskovit, Leonard. 1977. "Horace's Soracte Ode as a Poetic Representation of an Experience." *Studies in Philology* 74:113–29.

Mullin, Anne. 1990. "Revisiting the Soracte Ode." *New England Classical Newsletter and Journal* 17:24–25.

Mulroy, David. 1971–72. "Horace's Soracte Ode (I,9)." *CB* 48:77–80.

Murray, Michael. 1981. "Horace's Soracte Ode (I.9): The Hermeneutic Response." In Kresic 1981, 281–85.

Musurillo, Herbert. 1961. *Symbol and Myth in Ancient Poetry*. New York: Fordham University Press.

Nauck, A. ed. 1889. *Tragicorum graecorum fragmenta*. 2d ed. Leipzig: Teubner.

Nohl [first name not given]. 1915. "Zu Horaz carm. I.9." *Wochenschrift für klassische Philologie*, no. 1:20–22.

Nussbaum, G. 1965. "Some Notes on Symbolism in Horace's Lyric Poetry." *Latomus* 24:133–43.

Nutting, H. C. 1933. "Horace, Carmina 1.9.13–18." *CW* 26:147–48.

Oltramare, André. 1948. "En marge de quelques odes d'Horace." In *Mélanges de philologie, de littérature et d'histoire anciennes offerts à J. Marouzeau*, no editor, 457–63. Paris: Les Belles Lettres.

Otis, Brooks. 1970. "The Relevance of Horace." *Arion* 9:145–74.

Page, Denys. 1955. *Sappho and Alcaeus: An Introduction to the Study of Ancient Lesbian Poetry.* Oxford: Clarendon Press.

——, ed. 1974. *Supplementum lyricis graecis: Poetarum lyricorum graecorum fragmenta quae recens innotuerunt.* Oxford: Clarendon Press.

Palmer, H. R. 1911. *List of English Editions and Translations of Greek and Latin Classics Printed before 1641.* London: Blades, East and Blades.

Palmer, Richard E. 1981. "Horace's Soracte Ode (I.9): Philosophical Hermeneutics and the Interpretation." In Kresic 1981, 293–98.

Paratore, E. 1973. "La problematica sull'epicureismo a Roma." *ANRW* 1.4:116–204. Berlin.

Pasquali, Giorgio. 1920. *Orazio lirico.* Reprinted 1966, with introduction, indexes, and bibliographical appendix by Antonio La Penna. Florence: Felice Le Monnier.

Pease, Arthur Stanley, ed. 1920. "M. Tulli Ciceronis de divinatione liber primus." *Illinois Studies in Language and Literature* 6.2:2–338.

Plüss, Hans Theodor. 1882. *Horazstudien: Alte und neue Aufsätze.* Leipzig: Teubner.

Pollard, A. W., and G. R. Redgrave. 1986. *A Short-Title Catalogue of Books Printed in England, Scotland, and Ireland and of English Books Printed Abroad, 1475–1640.* Vol. 1. 2d ed., revised by W. A. Jackson and F. S. Ferguson and completed by Katharine F. Pantzer. London: The Bibliographical Society.

Porter, David H. 1987. *Horace's Poetic Journey: A Reading of Odes 1–3.* Princeton: Princeton University Press.

Pöschl, Viktor. 1966. "Die Soracte-ode des Horaz." *WS* 79:365–83. Reprinted in Pöschl, *Horazische Lyrik*, 30–51. Heidelberg: C. Winter, 1970. Also reprinted in *Antike Lyrik*, 217–37. Darmstadt: Wissenschaftliche Buchgesellschaft, 1970. My references are to *Horazische Lyrik*.

——. 1986. "Die Einführung des Liebesthema in den Horazischen 'Paradeoden.'" In *Kontinuität und Wandel. Lateinische Poesie von Naevius bis Baudelaire. Franco Munari zum 65. Geburtstag,* ed. U. J. von Stache, W. Maaz, and F. Wagner, 63–69. Hildesheim: Weidmann.

Quinn, Kenneth. 1980. "The Poet and His Audience in the Augustan Age." *ANRW* 2.30.1:75–180.

Quint, Maria-Barbara. 1987. *Untersuchungen zur mittelalterlichen Horaz-Rezeption.* Studien zur klassischen Philologie, no. 39. Frankfurt am Main: Peter Lang.

Reiff, Arno. 1959. *Interpretatio, Imitatio, Aemulatio: Begriff und Vorstellung literarischer Abhängigkeit bei den Römern.* Würzburg: K. Triltsch.

Rettig, J. W. 1965–66. "Dissolve frigus." *Classical Bulletin* 42:19–23.

Rider, Henry. 1644. *All the Odes and Epodes of Horace.* London: Richard Cotes.

Rösler, Wolfgang. 1980. *Dichter und Gruppe: Eine Untersuchung zu den Bedingungen und zur historischen Funktion früher griechischen Lyrik am Beispiel Alkaios.* Munich: Wilhelm Fink.

Rudd, Niall. 1960. "Patterns in Horatian Lyric." *AJP* 81: 373–92.

Ryle, Gilbert. 1949. *The Concept of Mind.* Chicago: University of Chicago Press.

St. John, Jack. 1972. "Horace, Odes I,9." *Echos du monde classique* = *Classical Views* 16:4–11.

Sandys, J. E. 1903–8. *A History of Classical Scholarship.* Cambridge: Cambridge University Press.

Santirocco, Matthew S. 1986. *Unity and Design in Horace's Odes.* Chapel Hill: University of North Carolina Press.

Schmalzriedt, Egidius. 1970. *ΠΕΡΙ ΦΥΣΕΩΣ: Zur frühgeschichte der Buchtitel.* Munich: Wilhelm Fink.

Segal, Charles. 1981. "Horace's Soracte Ode (I.9): Of Interpretation, Philologic and Hermeneutic." In Kresic 1981, 287–92.

Seidensticker, Bernd. 1976. "Zu Horaz, C. 1.9." *Gymnasium* 83:26–34.

Setaioli, Aldo. 1981. "Gli 'Epodi' di Orazio nella Critica dal 1937 al 1972." *ANRW* 2.31.3:1674–1788.

Shackleton Bailey, D. R. 1982. *Profile of Horace.* Cambridge: Harvard University Press.

Shields, M. G. 1958. "Odes 1.9: A Study in Imaginative Unity." *Phoenix* 12:166–73.

Smereka, Johannes. 1930–31. "Die artificiosa Horatii contaminatione (ad C. I9)." *Eos* 33:311–21.

Springer, Carl P. E. 1988. "Horace's Soracte Ode: Location, Dislocation, and the Reader." *CW* 82:1–9.

Stemplinger, E. 1913. "Horatius." In *Real-Encyclopädie der klassischen Altertumswissenschaft* 8:2336–99. Ed. A. Pauly, G. Wissowa, and W. Kroll, 1893–.

Sullivan, G. C. 1963. "Horace: Odes I,9." *AJP* 84:290–94.

Sullivan, J. P. 1981. "Horace's Soracte Ode (I.9): The Philological Aspects." In Kresic 1981, 277–80.

Tchernia, André. 1986. *Le vin de l'Italie: Essai d'histoire économique d'après les amphores.* Paris: Bibliothèque des Ecoles Françaises d'Athènes et de Rome. Fasc. 261.

Terranova, A. 1974. "Metafora e struttura nell'ode I,9 di Orazio." *Siculorum Gymnasium* 27:1–17.

Teuffel, W. S., et al. 1920. *Geschichte der römischen Literatur.* 7th ed. Revised by Wilhelm Kroll and Franz Skutsch. Leipzig: Teubner. Reprinted Aalen: Scientia Verlag, 1965.

Thieme, P. 1972. "Sprachmalerei." *Zeitschrift für vergleichende Sprachforschung* 86:64–81.

Tiles, Mary. 1989. "Philosophy and the Analogies of Time." *Philosophical Forum* 20:182–94.

Toll, H. C. 1955. "Unity in the *Odes* of Horace." *Phoenix* 9:153–69.

Vessey, D. W. T. 1985. "From Mountain to Lovers' Tryst: Horace's Soracte Ode." *JRS* 75:26–38.

Voigt, Eva-Maria, ed. 1971. *Sappho et Alcaeus.* Amsterdam: Athenaeum - Polak and Van Gennep.

Vretska, Helmut. 1980. "Horaz c. 1.9—Versuch einer Annäherung." *Der altsprachliche Unterricht* 23:23–39.

Weise, Oscar. 1882. *Die griechischen Wörter im Latein.* Leipzig: S. Hirzel.

West, David. 1967. *Reading Horace.* Edinburgh: Edinburgh University Press.

———. 1973. "Horace's Poetic Technique in the 'Odes.'" In Costa 1973, 29–58.

West, M. L., ed. 1971. *Iambi et elegi graeci ante Alexandrum cantati.* Oxford: Clarendon Press.

Wilamowitz, Ulrich von. 1913. *Sappho und Simonides.* Berlin: Weidmann. Reprinted 1966.

Wilkinson, L. P. 1945. *Horace and His Lyric Poetry.* 2d ed. (1951). Cambridge: Cambridge University Press. Reprinted 1968, 1979. Cf. Copley 1946.

Williams, Gordon. 1968. *Tradition and Originality in Roman Poetry.* Oxford: Oxford University Press.

———. 1980. *Figures of Thought in Roman Poetry.* New Haven and London: Yale University Press.

Witke, E. C. 1963. "Varro and Horace Carm. I,9." *CP* 58:112–15.

Chronological List of Works on Odes 1.9

1765 or after (1910) Galiani, Ferdinando. *Gli studi sopra Orazio dell'abate Ferdinando Galiani.* Ed. Fausto Nicolini. Naples: Francesco Giannini e Figli. See Nicolini's introduction, especially p. xv, for the reconstruction of Galiani's observations.

1840 Düntzer, H. *Kritik und Erklärung der horazischen Gedichte,* Part 1 (Die Oden),

171–74. Braunschweig: G. C. E. Meyer. Düntzer refers, by last name only, to discussions of the ode by seven predecessors: Döring, Grävius, Hippel, Jacobs, Ramler, Sanadon, and Vanderbourg. The Hippel to whom Düntzer refers is probably Theodor Gottlieb von Hippel (1741–96), a man of letters. I have not been able to ascertain in which of his works he discusses Horace. The Sanadon to whom he refers published a translation of Horace, with comments, in 1756. For Döring and Grävius, see Editions and Commentaries. I have no information on Jacobs, Ramler, and Vanderbourg. Jacobs and Sanadon are mentioned in the preface of Döring 1831, along with several others not mentioned by Düntzer: Bentley, Cunningham, Jani, Lambinus, Mitscherlich, Sparr, Torrentius, Wakefield, and Wetzel.

1841 Dillenburger, W. Quaestionum Horatianarum Particula I. et II., 37–39. Bonn: Habicht.

1843 Düntzer, H. Kritik und Erklärung der horazischen Gedichte, Part 3 (Die Episteln), 15–17. Braunschweig: G. C. E. Meyer. He agrees with Dillenburger (38) that cetera refers to politics. He discusses the date of the composition of the ode in relation to Epod. 13.

1846 Düntzer, H. Kritik und Erklärung der horazischen Gedichte, Part 5 (Nachträge und Berichtigungen), 27–28. Braunschweig: G. C. E. Meyer. He cites the discussion of the end of the ode by Galiani.

1881 Kiessling, Adolf. "Horatius." Philologische Untersuchungen 2:48–122 at 62–63.

1882 Plüss, Hans Theodor. Horazstudien: Alte und neue Aufsätze, 44–76. Leipzig: Teubner.

1901 Merrill, E. T. "Horace, Carm I.9.1 and I.2.14." CR 15:128–29.

1913 Wilamowitz, Ulrich von. Sappho und Simonides, 311. Berlin: Weidmann. Reprinted 1966.

1915 Nohl [first name not given]. "Zu Horaz carm. I.9." Wochenschrift für klassische Philologie, no. 1:20–22.

1920 Pasquali, Giorgio. Orazio lirico, 75–86. Reprinted 1966, with introduction, indexes, and bibliographical appendix by Antonio La Penna. Florence: Felice Le Monnier.

1924 Campbell, Archibald Y. Horace: A New Interpretation, 225. London: Methuen.

1925 Birt, Theodor. Horaz' Lieder und römisches Leben, 35–38. Leipzig: Quelle and Meyer.

1926 Burger, C. P. Aere Perennius: Scherts en Ernst in de Oden van Horatius, 137–43.

The Hague: M. Nijhoff. I have not seen this book. Henderson 1967, 13 n. 4: Burger assumes "that this ode was an answer to a poem by Thaliarchus complaining of the cold."

1930–31 Smereka, Johannes. "Die artificiosa Horatii contaminatione (ad C. I9)." *Eos* 33:311–21.

1933 Nutting, H. C. "Horace, Carmina 1.9.13–18." *CW* 26:147–48.

1935 Fairclough, H. R. *Some Aspects of Horace.* San Francisco: Privately printed. Cited by MacKay (1977) as the basis of his interpretation of the place (Rome) and the time (end of March) of the poem's setting. I have not seen Fairclough.

1943 Keseling, Paul. "Homerica." *Philologische Wochenschrift* 63:141–42.

1945 Wilkinson, L. P. *Horace and His Lyric Poetry.* 2d ed. (1951), 129–31. Cambridge: Cambridge University Press. Reprinted 1968, 1979. Cf. Copley 1946.

1946 Copley, F. O. Review of Wilkinson 1945. *AJP* 67:280–83.

1948 Oltramare, André. "En marge de quelques odes d'Horace." In *Mélanges de philologie, de littérature et d'histoire anciennes offerts à J. Marouzeau,* no editor, 457–63. Paris: Les Belles Lettres. Negligible.

1950 Hommel, Hildebrecht. *Horaz: Der Mensch und das Werk,* 97–99. Heidelberg: F. H. Kerle. On word order of last stanza.

1951 Hommel, Hildebrecht. "Cetera Mitte: Zu Archilochos, Horaz, Euripides und Empedokles." *Gymnasium* 58:218–27. Illustrations of *permitte divis cetera.*

1954 Bagnani, G. "No Fire without Smoke!," *Phoenix* 8:23–27.

1955 Molina, M. "Horacio, Carm. I,9 Vides ut alta . . ., versión y comentario." *Palaestra Latina* 149:27–32. I have not seen this article.

1955 Toll, H. C. "Unity in the Odes of Horace." *Phoenix* 9:153–69 at 162–63.

1957 Cunningham, M. P. "*Enarratio* of Horace Odes 1.9." *CP* 52:98–102.

1957 Fraenkel, Eduard. *Horace,* 176–77. Oxford: Oxford University Press.

1957 Highet, Gilbert. *Poets in a Landscape,* 122–23. New York: Knopf.

1958 Shields, M. G. "Odes 1.9: A Study in Imaginative Unity." *Phoenix* 12:166–73.

1959 Blaiklock, E. M. "The Dying Storm: A Study in the Imagery of Horace." *G&R,* n.s. 6:205–10.

1960 Rudd, Niall. "Patterns in Horatian Lyric." *AJP* 81:373–92.

1961 Collinge, N. E. *The Structure of Horace's Odes,* 65–67. London: Oxford University Press.

1961 Musurillo, Herbert. *Symbol and Myth in Ancient Poetry*, 137–38. New York: Fordham University Press.

1962 Commager, Steele. *The Odes of Horace*, 269–73. New Haven and London: Yale University Press.

1962 Delaunois, Marcel. "Paradoxes et subtilités d'Horace dans les odes du livre premier." *Les études classiques* 30:167–79 and 268–82 at 175–76.

1962 Gelsomino, R. "Leggendo l'ode del Soracte (Horat. Carm. I,9)." *Helikon* 2:553–71.

1963–64 Baneke, F. X. J. "De klanken van de Soracte." *Hermeneus* 35:262–65.

1963 Sullivan, G. C. "Horace: Odes I,9." *AJP* 84:290–94.

1963 Witke, E. C. "Varro and Horace Carm. I,9." *CP* 58:112–15.

1964 Avery, W. T. "Homeric Hospitality in Alcaeus and Horace." *CP* 59:107–9.

1964 Cunningham, J. V. *The Journal of John Cardan. Together with "The Quest of the Opal" and "The Problem of Form,"* 34–36 and 52–53. Denver: Alan Swallow. The copyright on "The Quest of the Opal: A Commentary on *The Helmsman*," which contains the pages on C. 1.9, is dated 1950.

1965 Cupaiuolo, F. "L'Ode I,9 di Orazio." *RSC* 13:278–86.

1965 Nussbaum, G. "Some Notes on Symbolism in Horace's Lyric Poetry." *Latomus* 24:133–43.

1965–66 Rettig, J. W. "Dissolve frigus." *Classical Bulletin* 42:19–23.

1966 Pöschl, Viktor. "Die Soracte-ode des Horaz." *WS* 79:365–83. Reprinted in Pöschl, *Horazische Lyrik*, 30–51. Heidelberg: C. Winter, 1970. Reprinted again in *Antike Lyrik*, 217–37. Darmstadt: Wissenschaftliche Buchgesellschaft, 1970. My references are to *Horazische Lyrik*.

1967 Henderson, W. J. "Horace, Carm. I.9: An Analysis." *Acta Classica* 10:11–18.

1967 Klinz, A. "Horaz, Carm. I,9—Catull, Carm. 5: Deutung und Vergleich." *Der altsprachliche Unterricht* 10.1:34–41.

1967 West, David. *Reading Horace*. Edinburgh: Edinburgh University Press.

1968–69 Esler, C. C. "Horace's Soracte Ode: Imagery and Perspective." *CW* 62:300–305.

1968 Lockyer, Jr., C. W. "Horace Odes I,9." *CJ* 63:304–8.

1968 Williams, Gordon. *Tradition and Originality in Roman Poetry*, 635–36. Oxford: Oxford University Press.

1969 Lee, M. Owen. *Word, Sound, and Image in the Odes of Horace*, 25–28. Ann Arbor: University of Michigan Press.

1970 Cunningham, J. V. "Odes I,9 and a Note from the Quest of the Opal." *Arion* 9:175–77. Cunningham's translation of C. 1.9 and reprint of a passage from Cunningham 1964.

1970 Otis, Brooks. "The Relevance of Horace." *Arion* 9:145–74.

1971–72 Mulroy, David. "Horace's Soracte Ode (I,9)." CB 48:77–80.

1972 Connor, Peter. "Soracte Encore." *Ramus* 1:102–12.

1972 Haffter, H. "Die Soracte-Ode des Horaz (I,9)." MH 29:172–76.

1972 St. John, Jack. "Horace, Odes I,9." *Echos du monde classique* = *Classical Views* 16:4–11.

1972 Thieme, P. "Sprachmalerei." *Zeitschrift für vergleichende Sprachforschung* 86:64–81. Page 68 is on the last stanza of C. 1.9.

1973 West, David. "Horace's Poetic Technique in the 'Odes.'" In Costa 1973, 29–58 at 54–55. For Costa see *General Bibliography*.

1974 Terranova, A. "Metafora e struttura nell'ode I,9 di Orazio." *Siculorum Gymnasium* 27:1–17.

1976 Catlow, Laurence. "Fact, Imagination and Memory in Horace, Odes 1.9." G&R 23:74–81.

1976 Moritz, L. A. "Snow and Spring: Horace's Soracte Ode Once Again." G&R 23:169–76.

1976 Seidensticker, Bernd. "Zu Horaz, C. 1.9." *Gymnasium* 83:26–34.

1977 MacKay, L. A. "Horatiana: Odes 1.9 and 1.28." CP 72:316–18.

1977 Moskovit, Leonard. "Horace's Soracte Ode as a Poetic Representation of an Experience." *Studies in Philology* 74:113–29.

1980 Vretska, Helmut. "Horaz c. 1.9—Versuch einer Annäherung." *Der altsprachliche Unterricht* 23:23–39.

1980 Williams, Gordon. *Figures of Thought in Roman Poetry*, 200–204. New Haven and London: Yale University Press.

1981 Kresic, Stephanus, ed. *Contemporary Literary Hermeneutics and Interpretation of Classical Texts*. Ottawa: Ottawa University Press.

1981 Murray, Michael. "Horace's Soracte Ode (I.9): The Hermeneutic Response." In Kresic 1981, 281–85.

1981 Palmer, Richard E. "Horace's Soracte Ode (I.9): Philosophical Hermeneutics and the Interpretation." In Kresic 1981, 293–98.

1981 Segal, Charles. "Horace's Soracte Ode (I.9): Of Interpretation, Philologic and Hermeneutic." In Kresic 1981, 287–92.

1981 Sullivan, J. P. "Horace's Soracte Ode (I.9): The Philological Aspects." In Kresic 1981, 277–80.

1982 Minadeo, Richard. *The Golden Plectrum*, 19–22. Amsterdam: Rodopi.

1985 Fitzgerald, W. H. "Firewalking on Soracte: A Vergilian Note on Horace Carmen I.9." *Vergilius* 31:59–60.

1985 Vessey, D. W. T. "From Mountain to Lovers' Tryst: Horace's Soracte Ode." *JRS* 75:26–38.

1986 Santirocco, Matthew S. *Unity and Design in Horace's Odes*, 39–41. Chapel Hill: University of North Carolina Press.

1987 Gagliardi, Donato. "La barriera sottile del presente: Struttura e senso dell'ode oraziana I.9." *CCC* 8:199–208.

1988 Springer, Carl P. E. "Horace's Soracte Ode: Location, Dislocation, and the Reader." *CW* 82:1–9.

1989 Clay, Jenny Strauss. "Horace *Ode* 1.9: Horace's September Song." *CW* 83:102–5.

1990 Mullin, Anne. "Revisiting the Soracte Ode." *New England Classical Newsletter and Journal* 17:24–25.

Index of Ancient
Passages Cited

• • • • • • • • • • •

General Index

• • • • • • • • • • • •

DATE DUE